Praise for *Hope After Trauma a...*

Sydney Segen offers a clearly written an... *trauma. Her book explores this difficul... ...anging from war, child abuse, domestic abuse, and m... ...rises. Moreover, she focuses on the insights gleaned and the resilience gained from hardship. This book provides a valuable resource and a source of hope.*
—Dr. Arielle Schwartz, author of *The Complex PTSD Workbook*

Brimming with hope and helpful tips for how to live with the fallout from severe trauma and betrayal, Sydney Segen takes readers on an inspiring and heartbreaking journey into the worlds of those who struggle with PTSD.
—Laurie Hall, author of *An Affair of the Mind*

I just couldn't put this book down—I read it all in one sitting. I learned that the behaviors I see in a friend are like symptoms of PTSD. Now I understand.
—Bonni Engel

Sydney Segen writes from her heart and her head, bringing together personal experiences with practical, sound strategies for dealing effectively with PTSD. Her honest sharing is both gripping and encouraging. She invites her readers to grow with her—an act of empathic compassion. When you read this book, you will meet a victor in its author.
—Laura Warfel, writer and author

The book was beautifully written and well organized. I pray that those who read this book will find solace in knowing they are not alone. I must admit that some sections of the book were very painful to read, as they brought to light many issues I thought I had successfully dealt with.
—M.T.

Ms. Segen's book doesn't give you a chance to put it down; it grabs you and doesn't let go until she clearly shows you the path through your own experiences or the experiences of those you seek to help and understand. A saving grace to those afflicted by this crazy world we dwell in.
— JDC, RN, St. Louis, MO

I would recommend this book as a useful tool toward recovery for anyone suffering from PTSD. The content is heartfelt and thought provoking, making it a relevant reading for those hoping to find healing from past trauma.
—Susan Werner, Stephen Ministry leader

I learned a lot about different types of trauma, what PTSD is, and how it affects your whole life. I so appreciate how Sydney offers hope for change through God, and how He uses trusted friends, counselors, support groups, and His Word to facilitate healing.
—Joann Lewis

This book is about the need to lament—to live in the lament and not run from it—yet to lament with hope because of God's redeeming work in and through every circumstance in life. I pray that all who read it will embrace both the lament and the hope.
—Rev. Margie Swenson

Working through trauma takes commitment, healthy tools, and a community of safe, loving people to walk with you. Sydney worked hard, used the resources around her, developed a healthy community and worked through the trauma of her past. I pray that many will be touched by this book and the art of journaling. You have a story to tell! So start telling it. It needs to be told!
—Coach Katherine, A Circle of Joy Ministry

This book helped me know that I'm not alone.
—Sharon, reader and PTSD survivor

Acknowledgments

I could never have written this book without the essential help of many friends, family members, and professionals. First, I humbly thank the individuals who wrote their stories for this book. It was a difficult task in so many ways, and you were courageous to look back at the pain so others could understand PTSD better. You did a great job!

Thank you to my counselors, coaches, and psychiatrists for helping me move forward in my recovery from PTSD. Thank you to the prayer warriors in my life for both consistent prayer along the way and dramatic prayer when needed. Thank you to the Stephen Ministry organization at my church, and especially my personal Stephen Minister. Although I was in pieces much of the time, you kept guiding me and believing in me.

Thank you to special friends who supported me professionally and personally. Thank you to the many friends who read the book in draft form and gave me feedback. My dear family, you were there for me from the beginning, understanding me, welcoming me to a new home, and replacing sorrow with joy. Lastly, thank you to my wonderful editor, who gave this book, and me, a huge dose of hope.

Hope After
Trauma and PTSD

Making Sense of the Pain

Sydney Segen

Thank you for purchasing this book. A portion of the proceeds
are donated to the National Center for PTSD for their work
supporting U.S. veterans.

www.SydneySegen.com

Dedication:

To my sister,

Who bore the brunt of the abuse in our family,

But was determined to survive anyway.

And

To my faithful companion

I meant to rescue you; but it was you who rescued me.

Table Of Contents

Preface

Every journey has a starting point and a destination

I started this book deep in the clutches of PTSD (Post-Traumatic Stress Disorder). But as I wrote, I grew in my ability to handle the symptoms. In my research I learned facts and strategies to combat the flashbacks, fears, and nightmares.

Ultimately, I finished my story and gathered more stories from people who have experienced trauma in their lives. Writing our stories helps process the hurt and brokenness we've experienced and helps us put these painful things in the past.

I want to know your story, too. Are you on a similar path? If so, I want you to tell you that there's hope.

If you're having difficulty recovering from a loss, shock, or other tragedy—or if you know someone who is having difficulty—I invite you on this journey toward a productive future that holds hope and joy for you.

How can this book help you?

First, you'll likely find some similarities between the people who wrote the featured stories and yourself. You'll notice differences, too. I chose these stories and their writers as representatives of some of the ways people encounter trauma. If the stories and information strike a chord with you, I hope you'll stay with us. The storytellers and I are with you in the midst of brokenness, and we're walking toward hope.

Second, after each story you'll see some insights about topics brought up by the story. Sometimes you'll find tips for dealing with difficulties, and always you'll be in the company of a writer who has experienced trauma and PTSD. I hope the insight sections arm you not only with knowledge, but also with the realization that *somebody understands me.*

Third, at the end of each section, you'll see an opportunity to answer questions and begin to write your own story. I hope you'll use all these places to interact with this book. Writing often helps people heal.

Fourth, you can get to know me and others who are on the journey to wholeness. I welcome your comments on my website, SydneySegen.com, on my Facebook page, and in our private Facebook group. I'll look forward to meeting you there.

Please take note
I'm a writer. I am not a clinician or an expert on PTSD and trauma. So any advice I give you is filtered through what experts recommend and what makes sense to me. Also, unless otherwise noted, the names, places, and situations in the stories have been altered for confidentiality.

Trigger warning
The stories in this book are true stories by people who have PTSD or PTSD symptoms. Some of the events in the stories might trigger flashbacks or a PTSD flare-up. If you have experienced trauma or have PTSD, please take note. If something you read triggers you, you could skip to the next section or stop reading for a few minutes to regain your composure.

Welcome to the journey.
Sydney

Introduction to Trauma and Post-Traumatic Stress Disorder (PTSD)

The attack was over. The damage had been done. The wounds had, for the most part, healed. I look like a normal person again, *thought Andres, staring in the mirror.* Then why can't I stay at work a whole day? Why is my brain is in a fog? I can't focus! Why don't I want to be around anyone anymore? *Disappointed in himself, but not able to pull out of the slump, Andres went back to bed, the only place that felt safe anymore.*

Have you had an event in your life that you just can't recover from? Do you know a friend or loved one who seems to be suffering endlessly from something that's happened in life?

It's possible that you or your friend have, like Andres, experienced trauma—an attack, a catastrophe, tragedy, or other shocking event that stopped life in its tracks. Many people who experience trauma get over it in a few weeks or months. But others just can't get their lives back together. Some of these people, including me and perhaps you, have Post-Traumatic Stress Disorder (PTSD).

If you have PTSD, you know how hard it is for others to understand what you're going through. They say, "Let go of the past." You say, "The past won't let go of me."

The true stories and insights about trauma and PTSD in this book assure you that others do understand your pain, and that you can begin to make sense of it—the first step toward healing. Making sense of the pain means taking a close, hard look at what happened to you and what has happened since. It means telling or writing about the pain, something I'll help you do with exercises at the end of each section in this book.

A high-level look at PTSD and trauma

Everyone who experiences trauma—such as war, abuse, loss of a loved one, a tragic accident, a crime—also experiences stress reactions to the trauma. Some people resolve this stress within a few weeks or months. Others don't. Either way, the traumatic event must be addressed, and symptoms of PTSD may occur.

Trauma and PTSD are formidable foes. They can break up marriages, cause people to lose jobs, rob people of mental and physical health. They can destroy life as you once knew it. If you or a loved one has experienced trauma or PTSD, you have my deepest empathy. I understand the loss, the unfairness, and the feelings of craziness because I also have PTSD. It's not a journey that we chose, but we can walk through it together.

One group of people seem to have more difficulty with PTSD than others: those who believe in God. Surprised? They can be in more agony over trauma and PTSD than everyone else because they have more questions. "How could God allow this? Why doesn't He heal me? Did He forget about me?"

I asked those same questions, and I've figured out a few answers with much help and many resources. While it's true that God can miraculously heal PTSD, a hoped-for miracle is not something to count on. But while you're waiting, you can take action yourself and allow God to heal you through therapy, medicine, and a safe support network. I sometimes half-jokingly say, "I needed prayer, Prozac, and people to get a handle on PTSD."

You'll learn much more about PTSD and trauma in the following pages. So get ready to walk together to make sense of the pain. The best is yet to come.

Section A

Trauma and PTSD from War Experiences

"No! Stop!" Joel shouted. It was four a.m. and Joel was safe in his bedroom, although the sheets and blankets on the bed looked like a war zone. He dropped back onto his pillow. Not again, he thought. Joel had awoken from another PTSD-driven nightmare in which he relived the hand-to-hand, life-and-death combat he'd experienced in Iraq. Even before the war, Joel had been deathly afraid of being injured, having grown up as a punching bag for his relentless older brothers. Reliving the dream and the combat experience, Joel's heart was so heavy he couldn't see how to get through the day.

PTSD: Who is at risk?

Joel is suffering from Post-Traumatic Stress Disorder (PTSD). The traumatic stress of battle, physical or emotional abuse, natural disaster, and all other types of tragedies put people at risk of getting PTSD. Yet not everyone who goes to war or experiences catastrophes develops PTSD.

The following lists show a few indicators of who is more or less likely to develop clear symptoms. Don't be concerned if you frequently find yourself in the "More Likely" column. This isn't a diagnosis, it's merely a reminder that taking a look at our lives is a good place to start a healing journey.

LESS LIKELY to develop PTSD after trauma	MORE LIKELY to develop PTSD after trauma
People with a stable family background and healthy attachments to parents and other early caregivers	People who have early family instability and disorganized attachment styles often grow up with fewer skills and less experience in coping with difficult circumstances
Individuals with no prior exposure to trauma or chronically stressful life experiences	People who are already dealing with trauma or chronic stress find their coping mechanisms stretched to, and perhaps beyond, the capacity to handle more trauma
People who are in a good state of mental health	People with prior affective, anxiety, or substance abuse disorders have fewer internal resources and less healthy habits to survive a new stressor
Men rather than women	Women may be more susceptible as a group because they are more vulnerable to assaults by stronger members of the opposite sex
People who have the character quality of "resilience"	Just as some people are physically less resistant to diseases, people who are mentally or emotionally less resilient have a harder time bouncing back after trauma
People with a support network	People who have no one "in their corner" after trauma feel more alone, tend to isolate more, and avoid reaching out for help

If you found yourself in the "More Likely" list above, please don't be alarmed. Most people will relate to something in that list. This is not a judgment call; it's simply a way to better understand who is more susceptible. People in the "Less Likely" column are also not immune to PTSD. Keep this list in mind as you get to know Doug, the author of our first story.

War and PTSD

This section contains a real-life battle story. I want you to be aware that it's graphic, contains profanity, and will have you on the edge of your seat.

Some people find this story too difficult to read because it "triggers" (brings back) memories or flashbacks (reliving experiences) of similar situations. If that's true for you, try taking breaks from the story as you read it. You may need to skip the story altogether, especially if you've been in the military. That's okay. As you progress with the book and writing exercises, you may feel strong enough to return to this powerful story.

Why this story is the first one

All men and women who are called to military duty put their very lives on the line, sometimes losing that life, and always coming away changed. They're heroes, and there is always a cost. The sheer numbers of military personnel who have PTSD have brought this condition to the world's attention. Since the Vietnam War, and based on military personnel's sacrifices, the diagnosis of Post-Traumatic Stress Disorder has been identified and formally recognized. Now people in all walks of life can receive earlier diagnoses and better treatment. The National

Center for PTSD[1] says:

> The PTSD diagnosis has filled an important gap in psychiatry in that its cause was the result of an event the individual suffered, rather than a personal weakness.

As you read, remember that these stories are not about weakness, failure, or "trying harder." The stories are about *something that happened* and caused PTSD to develop in a person's life.

And now, the story of a hero, in his own words.

I Keep Biting That Same Bullet

Doug, in his own words

The irony is that, as a kid, I never even had a Daisy air rifle. Maybe a pea-shooter in third grade to aggravate the girls. Do my pre-teen squirt guns count? How 'bout my Colt M16A—the infamous black rifle of the green jungle? Not exactly for hunting deer.

And my first firefight, a gunfight. A play-for-keeps gunfight seven kilometers from the Cambodian border. This was just the end of my second week in South Vietnam.

We were supposed to have the day off, too! It was our company's day to stay back at the firebase. Our turn to guard the fort. Clean our weapons. Write home. Catch up on sleep. Easy day, for sure. Maybe the mid-afternoon mail chopper will bring me my first letter from home. From Julie. From Mom. Anybody.

But easy-time lasted until late morning when some E6-type career platoon sergeant, a "lifer," came scrambling along the bunker line grabbing one or two guys from each bunker—those sandbagged holes we lived in—while barking orders to get our asses down to the chopper line pronto, and bring our shit. Our gear. Our stuff. And full ammo.

All this started after one of our observation helicopters got hit by North Vietnamese ground fire and went down about 10 chopper-minutes from our firebase at Katum.

Katum. That's one of those words that came home with me.

Anyway, this was all new to me. After almost two weeks I had not fired one freakin' shot. No one had. So where's this war everyone's bitching about back home?

But this was January 5, 1968. Three more words that came home with me. They share the top spot. No. They own it, actually.

We had to secure that downed chopper and check for survivors or retrieve bodies. That crazed staff sergeant running along the bunker line was able to round up about a "hunnert" of us who were supposed to have the day off. I didn't expect him to need that many of us, but what did I know? I was a "greenie." A battle virgin just short of two weeks in country.

Yet there it was. Some guys I'd never met got shot down out of the sky and they needed us.

We all double-timed a couple hundred yards to the chopper pad where eight Huey Slicks impatiently whined and "thwaaaked-thwaaaked." They sound different on the ground. I was eating up the excitement, and my adrenalin told me so. Fifty years later I still look up when I hear a helicopter. Any kind. I watch them all. Sort of stayed with me.

Ten minutes later I was dangling my just-turned-twenty-year-old legs a thousand feet above what could have been mistaken for Iowa farmland, but greener. My new jungle combat boots still looked relatively fresh and stood out from the others.

We did a tight 180, and quickly dropped into a cold LZ—a quiet landing zone free of the bad guys (so we thought) in a clearing a few hundred yards from the downed chopper.

You have to understand the numbers here because those numbers determine how quickly we get in and how quickly we get out. X number of guys need X number of choppers to quickly get in and even more quickly get out.

We were the first of two insertions (guys landing)—eight choppers with eight guys per chopper. (Note the numbers.) And we had to wait for the second insertion of sixty-something more guys to join up with us before we all would head out. One-hundred twenty guys in four platoons—typically one company.

Until that second lift returns with the second half, lay low, keep your head down, and shut your mouth.

I was now in the first of two defensive perimeters which I hadn't planned on being in today.

Sure enough, about 20 minutes later those same eight Hueys came out of the sun, dropped down into the same LZ and dropped-off about sixty-something more of us in less time than you can say "LBJ." Instinct got us all to the woodline.

So there we were. A hundred or so armed-to-the-teeth bad-ass warriors—and me—securing the area so the recovery team could remove the dead crew from the dead chopper. I was armed to the teeth, but I was not yet a warrior. I had to earn that.

Fifteen minutes later I saw my first body bag carried out right past me. The silence was more solemn than a requiem high mass without the choir. No one had to tell me what was going on. *They're going home. Early.*

I then watched that E6-type shove a couple of magnesium-whatever thermite grenades up inside the chopper's avionics. The Pentagon didn't want our high-tech stuff making its way to those Chinese Commies, a suddenly convenient ally of the North Vietnamese Commies. That white-hot thermite melted the chopper's interior in less than two minutes. Never saw anything like that before.

So there we were. Done for the day. About 120 of us waiting our turn for the ten-minute chopper ride back to our firebase. Maybe I'll finally have some mail waiting for me.

But only four choppers returned for extraction—getting us out—because the other four were redeployed somewhere else. So instead of two return lifts of about 60 of us per lift, there would be four separate lifts of 30 each of us dudes going back to Katum. There's that word again.

We were also taken back in reverse order from which we arrived. (Don't ask.) That meant my group of 30 guys—first platoon—was the first one in and would now be the last one out.

I didn't give it a second thought. Not my job to make those decisions. Besides, what did I know?

Remember me asking you to remember the numbers? Stay with me here.

About 20 minutes after the fourth platoon was extracted, the choppers returned. Third platoon sprinted half a football field and jumped into the Hueys. Just like training at Fort Polk.

Sure enough, 20 minutes or so later it was second platoon's turn. Then they left.

So most of the company's gone, and 31 of us were stretched along the woodline, where the thick jungle starts, waiting our turn. Looking back on that, seems we were all lulled by nothing really going on. We kept quiet, though. Chatter here, chatter there, but low key. A few of the guys lit up. But we all kept looking into the woods. Actually, more like *hearing* into the woods. Couldn't see that far into it.

But it was our turn to get out, and the choppers were probably on their way back to pick us up.

Then I heard a twig snap to my direct front. Or, I thought I did. No, I did. Couldn't tell you how far in—maybe 30 or 40 feet, but I heard something. Sounded like someone stepped on a dry twig, or something rustled in the thick bush. It was quick. Then nothing. I waited a bit, but didn't hear it again. Yet I felt compelled to report it.

I stood up just enough to get my squad leader's attention, and waved him over. Eric Hansen from Minnesota, a blue-eyed blonde with Norwegian heritage who bragged about his Viking ancestors. Watched him scramble toward me, hunched-over just like in the war movies. I pointed into the bush and told him I heard something. He listened; we both listened. Nothing. We peered ahead, still listening. Couple of guys around us listened, too. Maybe 10 seconds. Nuttin'. But I didn't get hassled. He just told me to stay alert.

I'm tellin' ya, I heard something, and I'm going to my grave with that conviction.

Also heard the choppers coming back before we saw 'em. They fly directly over the treetops to minimize their exposure to ground fire possibly coming up from directly below.

Our turn to get out of here. *"Di di mau!"* (Let's go!) The four Bell UH-1D Iroquois helicopters once again curled into a tight 180 right behind one another, dropping down and hovering three feet off the ground about 40 or 50 yards directly out from the woodline.

I stayed even with the others as we dashed from the cover of the woodline to the choppers. Just like Fort Polk, Louisiana 71459. The door gunners sat on flack-jackets to avoid getting shot in the ass should ground fire come up through the chopper floor. Made sense to me.

We were more than halfway to the Hueys when the shit hit. The instantaneous, attention-getting bright orange flash to my right front had the ugliest instantaneous sound I've ever heard. Can't even begin to describe it. Then a few more—maybe three or four.

Just like that, all four Hueys pushed up, nosed down, and sprinted away. On their way out, door gunners filled both woodlines with continuous fire which wasn't that far over our heads. You don't see the fluorescent red tracers when they're coming at you, yet I knew that millisecond *"krraaaaak"* over my head was the real thing. This wasn't live-fire low-crawl in some Fort Polk mud pit. This is war.

Up and down the line I immediately heard, *"Get back! Get back! Get back!"* Out in the open and running in shin-deep grass, we sprinted back to the woodline. Incoming mortars left thin gray smoke all around us. Smoke just thick enough that I almost didn't see the body without a jaw. No jaw. What! People aren't supposed to look like that. What was left of the bottom half of his head was a cavity splayed open showing thoracic and upper chest stuff. His spine was shattered away from the base of his skull. I took in all of that in the second or two as I ran by. And I've never forgotten … I've been looking back ever since … images still in my head. One of the reasons I'm writing this.

Hector and a couple other guys were yelling and setting up our defensive perimeter. Half of us faced into the bush, and the other half set up looking across the open LZ, about as big as two or three football fields. Controlled chaos. Hector was our platoon leader, a gold bar Second Lieutenant. Hardly knew him. But in my short time in the field, I could tell he had his shit together.

Hector spent a lot of time on the "horn," the radio he pulled off the back of our dead radio guy. The radio's volume was maxed-out. Full squelch. Had to be. Hector was hunkered down over a map yelling grid coordinate stuff back to the firebase. I don't think a minute went by when the first of our big-ass artillery rounds came in and hit pretty freakin' close. We weren't that far from the receiving end of our own artillery trying to keep the enemy away from us. Proverbial cannon fodder? Hope not.

Bobby Harrington, one of the first guys I met when I arrived at my unit, shouted at me to get down behind the berm. I immediately dropped down. A few seconds later, Bobby's yelling at me while reaching over, grabbing my ammo belts and pulling me over to his side of the berm: the side *away* from the stuff coming at us. Still can't believe I set up on the wrong side of that berm. New guy mistake.

The highest point of that shallow and rolling berm was maybe a foot higher than my steel pot—my helmet. This was serious. And for the first time in my life I felt fear. The first time in my life I was scared. Really scared.

My left cheek was flat on the dirt. I looked to my right and saw a guy lying away from me on his left side. All I could see was that he was curled up with his hole-riddled backpack facing me and head down. Couldn't see his face so I didn't know who he was. He didn't move. His jungle fatigue top was darker than his jungle fatigue bottom. Blood darker. He didn't move. Every time I looked over at him, he did not move. Bobby Harrington said he was dead.

Beyond him I saw three North Vietnamese Regulars running along the edge of the woodline on the other side of the LZ. Maybe 100 yards from us. My first clear look at "the enemy." Two of the guys in front were pulling a big-wheeled cart with some sort of machine gun on it. Shit. It looked bigger than our squad's M-60s. A few more guys were running right behind that gun cart carrying their first generation AK-47s. It was obvious they were after us, and they had set things up.

All of this is going on what seemed only a few minutes into the fight. The shit started real quick and lasted real long.

Bobby Harrington's third or fourth shot from his grenade launcher hit just in front of that machine gun cart. I saw the flash and heard a "whumm." Not sure if that cart or those guys got back into the fight.

I laid down a base of fire for the very first time since advanced infantry at Fort Polk. This was the real thing and it wasn't cool to stick your head up and see how it was going. I'd click off short bursts of two or three rounds into the thick scrub or whatever you want to call it, duck down for a few seconds, and pop back up with another quick burst. Just doin' what the other guys were doin'. This shit's all new to me and I was scared.

Sometime during all of this, an LOH, a small Light Observation Helicopter called a "loach," buzzed treetop high, rapidly spitting softball-size air-to-ground grenades into those trees in the far woodline across the LZ. *"Fwooommp! Fwooommp! Fwooommp! Fwooommp!"* Must've made three or four passes that kept the enemy pinned down for a while.

Word came down the line to set up claymores—anti-personnel mines about the size of a two-inch-thick *Reader's Digest*, with spikes to anchor into the dirt. C4 plastic explosive on the back send 700 steel ball bearings screaming knee-high out the front, shredding everything in their way. Each of us carried at least two claymores. If they could, some guys felt safer carrying more. I looked over at Bobby who looked over at me and said "Let's go!" I crawled right behind Bobby over the top of the berm and down the other shallow side. We were exposed, but that "loach" was keeping enemy heads down across the LZ. We placed our claymores about 10 feet to our front and about 10 feet apart. Up and down the line, others were doing the same. Bobby and I rolled back over to the secure side of that berm, ready to pop those claymores if the NVA rushed us again.

Well, this has gotta come up sooner or later, so here goes. *Over the years, I have frequently been asked if I had killed anyone in Vietnam.* Yes, I have. But I'm not sure if I hit anyone at first. That finally came four or five magazines into the fight. I saw him go down. It wasn't anything like I imagined and certainly not like Hollywood. He fell down. Just suddenly collapsed and didn't move. Watched him for a moment—enough not to forget. Adrenalin then quickly took my attention to the other NVA, spread out and running right at us across the open LZ. They stopped when one of our guys opened up with his M-60. Then another squad gun opened-up into the woodline behind us seconds later. They were hitting us from all sides. We stayed flat and close to the ground.

Not sure how far we were into the fight, but the brightest white light I have ever seen pierced my eyes and blew into my head in a millisecond. I had never experienced an instant—any instant —like that. Something hit really close to me. Maybe 30 feet at most. I was looking in that direction when it happened, so I got it all. That flash was the brightest and purest white light I have ever seen. In a nanosecond, something brighter than the sun suddenly filled me, then suddenly left me. So white! So sudden that I don't remember the sound or the concussion. It was the light! Fifty years later, I still haven't seen anything like it.

I know I didn't say "ouch," but I remember making some kind of noise. Just happened, maybe a half-hour into the fight. A sudden pinch with something sharp that stayed with me. I just got shot in my right leg, up high near my hip. Not excruciating pain, but it hurt and it didn't stop. Neither did the bleeding. I rolled over on my left side and saw my fatigue pants getting darker on my right side. My fingers found the small hole in the darkest part of those fatigues. There it was. I couldn't believe I got hit. I freakin' got shot! Or something. At that moment, I wanted to make myself the smallest target possible, but it really hurt to bend my knee and pull my leg up toward my chest. "Medic!" I kept looking around. "Medic!" Emptied another magazine and still no medic. *Think, Doug!* Gave myself a spring-loaded injection of stuff into my right thigh that's supposed to coagulate things down there and stop the bleeding. Practiced this at Fort Polk—but didn't practice the fear. I had to defend myself, so I filled a few more mags and rolled over to return fire.

The dozen magazines on the ground around me were empty. Still a few full mags left. Also had a couple bandoliers of loose ammo for reloads. Shoving bullet after bullet by hand up into the empty magazines as fast as I could wasn't part of training at Fort Polk. Talk about pressure! Head down. Reload empty mags. Didn't see that North Vietnamese dude pop through the scrub until he saw me. I saw his face, and he saw my face. Fifty or 60 feet at most. Pitcher's mound to home plate. I was flat on my stomach loading my mags with my weapon next to me at the ready—*but not in hand.* And I wasn't as quick and nimble with the leg hit. So all he had to do was turn slightly, raise his AK, and take me out right then and there. Three seconds max. But I didn't know Roy Swan was to my left maybe 20 or 30 feet until he popped up from the high grass and shot that guy dead-in-the-head at close range. I saw it. The guy didn't. Three more seconds and he would have shot me dead. I just know it. I still see Roy dropping that guy ... I see it all ... one of my more frequent images. I'm used to it. If it weren't for Roy Swan, I wouldn't be here still seeing this same show running in my head every single day.

Hector was back on the horn again with the volume still maxed-out at full squelch. I heard the chopper's "thwaaak-thwaaaks" but could not make out what Hector and the pilot were saying in between my short, semi-automatic two- and three-round bursts. Lot of noise. But one of the guys lying closer to Hector heard something none of us wanted to hear, yet we passed along the "heads-up" anyway. A chopper circling overhead was providing Hector with sky updates on our fight below. Word quickly spread that there were about 300 NVA hitting us from two sides. Three "hunnert." There were 300 guys out there who wanted to kill the 31 of us.

This was it. I suddenly had a bad feeling about this—worse than when we first got hit, and even worse than when I got hit.

So there's a lot of shit still going on around us. Cobra gunships continuously pissed lead into the woodline across the LZ from where the main body of NVA would send small teams to penetrate our perimeter—just like that one guy Roy Swan took out.

I don't know why our battalion brass waited so long to do this, but several hours into this mess two McDonnel-Douglass F4 Phantoms showed up to the party with a few canisters of nasty napalm—high-octane, jellied gasoline. Barbequed NVA. Nothing like I have ever seen. The gunfire stopped immediately. What was left of the enemy ran the seven "klicks" or kilometers, back to Cambodia, with our Cobra gunships hot on their ass.

Now was our chance to get out! Hector quickly organized his able-bodies to bring our wounded and dead to the center of our perimeter, where quick counts were made and all were accounted for. Those unable to run were thrown over the shoulders of those who could. With a bullet in my leg, I was one of those who could not. I can't remember who carried me across the scarred LZ to the choppers, but I still owe that guy the most important beer in his life. He carried me past more bodies on our way out from our perimeter than there were bodies when we rushed into our perimeter three hours earlier. Someone picked up our man with no jaw. With the rotors straining, each chopper just below lift-off RPM, the door gunners jumped out and helped toss our seven dead and 14 wounded into bloody piles on their aircraft's floor. With all accounted for, the able-bodies jumped in and the door gunners let loose into both woodlines as we climbed our way out.

Twenty minutes or so later, Army surgical teams met all four choppers just yards away from their M.A.S.H. tents where I had my first taste of triage. O.R. medics pulled me off the bloody floor of the lead chopper and not-so-gently dropped my relieved ass on an Army-green canvas stretcher as someone gave me my first of several pain-killer injections. Some chaplain—I think he was a chaplain—met each stretcher coming into the O.R. tent and quickly determined who needed him and who did not need him. Not me, thank God! But his quick splash of holy water quenched my soul as a screaming and legless Eric Hanes was carried right past me. As two OR nurses cut off my bloody fatigues, I slowly faded to black under the gas-passer's most welcomed mask.

My life's worst day had come to its close.

PTSD: Thanks, Vietnam!

- Everything I've presented in this document regularly flies through my head unannounced in brief visions typically lasting no more than 10 seconds.
- Each vision reflects one of the paragraphs I've written on the previous pages, recreating its own vision unique to that paragraph.
- When I'm not completely focused on other matters, such visions appear in my mind several times every waking hour of every day.

- I have no control over when the visions appear, but I'm able to push them out rather easily; yet I know they'll surely return sooner than later.
- I'm used to it … this has been going on inside my head for the past 50 years.
- I'm convinced they'll continue appearing in my head to the day I die.

PTSD: Anything can—and does—take my thoughts back to Vietnam.

Whenever I see a helicopter—any helicopter—I think about Vietnam.

Whenever I hear a helicopter—any helicopter—I think about Vietnam.

Whenever I hear the traffic copter on my car radio, I think about Vietnam.

A baseball diamond is about the size of our platoon's perimeter in that gunfight. Position thirty-one men along the edge of the outfield grass, facing out, and that's about the area we defended. Whenever I attend a St. Louis Cardinals baseball game at Busch Stadium, thoughts about Vietnam come through me more than a few times during that game. Sure enough—in between innings when, and for several seconds only—very few players are on the field. The players on the team that just made the third out are still in the dugout grabbing their gloves. The players on the team coming into their dugout are pickin' up their bats or chugging down water. During such brief moments, most of that infield is empty and bare. But my mind transforms it to scrub brush, high grass, and other thick tropical growth, and I see that same gunfight. It might happen only once that game, maybe twice, but I know those thoughts will slide into my head as sure as the seventh-inning stretch. It's not intentional … it just happens.

The company where I worked for almost 20 years was situated near the end of a small regional airport in the far western suburbs of Chicago. At the other end of the airport, police and state highway helicopters shared hangar and flight facilities. The flight paths for all helicopter traffic vectored directly overhead of our building and parking lot. Throughout the day—day after day after day—I watched choppers from both units fly directly toward my office windows, passing only a couple hundred feet above. It was the same "thwaaak-thwaaak." It didn't bother me, but it brought back images of helicopter gunship "thunder runs."

A most profound life change with God

I don't know how many people know the feeling of surrendering themselves completely to God. Until this battle, I had never called upon God like I called upon Him that January day in Vietnam.

Instead of praying, I "thought" my feelings directly to Him. It had nothing to do with religion. It had nothing to do with being Catholic. It had nothing to do with any of the prayers I memorized in first grade. This was completely different. An Our Father or a Hail Mary just didn't make sense.

My thoughts were going directly to Him. I completely bypassed all Catholic protocol. Didn't think of Jesus, didn't think of Mary—not even the Holy Ghost. I needed to talk to The Man. Flat out told Him that *"WE NEED TO TALK."* That's exactly what my mind spoke: *"**WE NEED TO TALK!**"* I told Him I *needed* His attention just like that. Now! I had to get this to Him immediately before I got shot again. That was my complete focus during those moments. I remember simply telling God that I believe in who or what He is—that I want to be with Him whatever happens next and wherever that may be. And that if He's going to do it—do it fast, quick, clean, and I don't want to feel it.

I then told Him with my utmost intent and fear for my life: *"Lord, I give myself to Thee."* If it was my turn, then I was ready. I wanted to be absolutely certain that He knew—that I knew—that He was in charge and that everything was His call. I was never more prepared to meet God than during those moments. All of this took maybe thirty seconds.

Since then, I've had little interest in Catholic devotions I had practiced from my childhood until that January afternoon in Vietnam, although I still respect them deeply. I attend Sunday Mass maybe once or twice a year, and not necessarily on a feast day. I get more from my faith talking directly. Hope He's not mad at me. I believe He understands. He's still my King.

I know what prayer is and what works for me. I've already had my audience with God, and I'm ready for whatever's next. He knows where I'm coming from, and I hope He's okay with my shortcomings, my faults, my frailties, and my failures. Since that January afternoon almost 50 years ago, I have talked to Him every day.

Advice from Doug

If you have PTSD, deal with it. Get help, find your own way, but don't ignore it. Remember that you can't change that it happened. When you think you can't go on, remember these words a chaplain shared with me: "Courage doesn't mean you aren't scared; it means you do it anyway."

***

Insights from Doug's story

I am so humbled and grateful to share Doug's story with you. I've come to learn that soldiers and veterans rarely share the events of their war experiences with people who have not been to war. We don't know what it's like, so we can't fully understand.

However, Doug, a talented professional writer, took us right with him through the worst day of his life. He gave us a chance to better understand what war is like.

I happen to know that Doug agonized over this story for many months. It cost him a great deal to go back and revisit every minute in that January afternoon. He did that for me and you, and for other veterans who can't do it—just so we understand better.

Trauma upon trauma

Vietnam veterans not only faced the trauma of war, but they also faced the trauma of returning home to a country sharply divided in its support of the war. Many veterans returned unnoticed, others returned to protests, and all returned to a mixture of confusion, guilt, anger, and remorse over their role in such a confused war. As a country, we did a great disservice to men who risked their lives doing what they were told to do.

Now, decades after the experience Doug described, he still has flashbacks and intrusive thoughts. Sometimes the flashbacks are triggered, for example, by hearing a helicopter or seeing bullet casings. But most often the intrusive pictures and thoughts simply pop into Doug's mind unbidden. Those of us with PTSD often say we have two minds operating out of one body. One mind is trying to deal with the images and thoughts to keep them at bay, while the other mind is trying to drive safely, play with grandchildren, run a meeting, and carry on other normal activities.

This is exhausting work, and fatigue often accompanies PTSD.

Statistics for veterans and PTSD

The U.S. Department of Veterans Affairs[2] estimates that PTSD afflicts:

- Almost 31 percent of Vietnam veterans
- As many as 10 percent of Gulf War (Desert Storm) veterans
- 13 percent of veterans of the war in Afghanistan
- 20 percent of Iraqi war veterans

Helpful tips for PTSD's mind invasions

If this is your reality—the past taking over your mind again and again, I'm sorry this is happening to you. Here are three things I've found effective in this battle for the mind:

- Fill your mind with other things: Listen to music, read, write, focus on a word puzzle, engage someone in conversation. Keeping your mind busy with active, positive thoughts and activities can squeeze out the PTSD flashbacks.
- When you're driving, trying to rest, or trying to relax, shout out those PTSD thoughts. Tell them to, "Leave now! You have no place here. I have put you in the past, now stay there!"
- If you really can't get your mind free, put your body to work. Paint, rake, garden, sew, swim, walk briskly, go on a bike ride, play tennis. Physical activities that require your concentration leave less room for PTSD to invade.

Some days you'll be more successful than others—hurray!! Take a victory lap, do a winner's dance, tell someone. You have a reason to celebrate. As you practice this over time, you will have more and more better days. You're a warrior now.

Your Story
What happened to you

Reading this book may help you realize that you have a story to tell, too. Telling your story can help you take steps toward better mental health because writing integrates both the logical and the creative parts of your brain. By adding logic to the emotional turmoil you may be going through, you will better process your story and, eventually, lay it to rest. Below you'll find directions for starting your story. You can write it, tell it, draw it, paint it, or make a photo collage. But at some point, try to write it out.

First step

The first step in writing your story is an easy one. Just answer the question "What happened to you?" Try to keep your answer to about 25 words at the very most.

Start at the hardest part

After you answer, "What happened?" your story will naturally start to unfold (in later chapters) as we continue to flesh it out.

- What happened that caused your life to stop in its tracks?
- What happened that made you realize you were in deep trouble?
- What happened that changed the course of your life?

Example

For example, Doug might say:
"I went to war and had no idea what I was in for."

Please take a few moments to write "what happened."

Section B
Trauma and PTSD from Addiction, Betrayal, and Childhood Abuse

The sudden cell phone ring startled Linda so much that she dropped her cup of coffee. Linda's nerves were on edge the rest of the morning, as she expected something else to pop up out of the blue and scare her again. Ever since she had seen her husband, Dale, embrace, kiss, and caress another woman, Linda's life had changed drastically. She was constantly on edge.

Linda also raged at Dale, sobbed uncontrollably, was sure he was calling and texting the other woman—and dreaded the hour when he came home from work. She felt sick when she was around him; having him home was claustrophobic. Things couldn't go on this way. She needed Dale to express remorse, promise never to stray again, and show her his devoted love. But he kept his distance. Maybe I need to leave. *Linda thought grimly.* Maybe permanently—or even eternally.

In this chapter, we'll look at symptoms caused by Post-Traumatic Stress Disorder. Everyone will see some familiar symptoms in this chapter, so don't be concerned if that's the case for you. Again, we're not aiming for a diagnosis, but just to find out where we see ourselves as we make progress recovering from trauma—and to be a better friend to those around us who are dealing with PTSD.

Why symptoms are important

Mental health professionals such as counselors, psychologists, and psychiatrists diagnose PTSD in part by noting the presence, severity, and persistence of specific symptoms. When you read the lists of general symptoms below, don't be surprised if some sound familiar.

Almost everyone has a few things on the list. Having these symptoms doesn't mean you have PTSD.

Physical	Emotional	Lifestyle
You may feel sick to your stomach, have headaches, dizziness, fatigue, chest pain, breathing problems, diarrhea, hives, or other unexplainable physical symptoms or pain	You may have nightmares, flashbacks (reexperiencing the event as if you're going through it again), anxiety, reduced confidence, irritability, emotional numbing, depression, jitters, memory blocks, feelings of excessive guilt or shame, or rages; you may feel "on alert" all the time, startling at the smallest noise or unexpected sight	You may have a hard time sleeping, focusing, getting along with others, trusting others, going out in public, being with friends or family; you may try to self-medicate with alcohol, drugs, shopping, or overeating; you may stop caring about cleanliness or your appearance; you may need to take a leave of absence from work

Do you see some of these symptoms in Linda's story? She was sick to her stomach, overly watchful, anxious, and depressed. She startled easily and was distrusting. These are common responses to trauma, and being betrayed is experienced by many people as trauma.

If you notice that some symptoms above are present in your life, it means you've taken an honest look at what's going on. Good for you! The first step in getting better is recognizing that something's wrong.

On the other hand, if the symptoms don't sound familiar to you, but you still have distress, I hope you'll consider the next recommendation anyway.

You and I are not qualified to diagnose PTSD

The only way to have PTSD diagnosed, or ruled out, is to see a mental health professional. Professionals follow specific guidelines in making diagnoses; any other method is just a guess.

It's a good idea to consider making an appointment at a clinic or with an individual if you have symptoms that have:

- Lasted longer than three months
- Caused you great distress
- Disrupted your home or work life

The story focus of this section: sexual trauma

You are about to meet two women who have experienced sexual trauma. You may be surprised at how each person handles the trauma.

One thing is true for both: The trauma and PTSD are so terrifying that these women know they can't stand still and survive. They must find some way to muscle through the events of the past and become healthier people who can successfully stay in the present. As you read the stories, look for some of the symptoms listed above.

The stories contain graphic descriptions and sexual abuse topics. If you find the stories too difficult to read, skip to the next chapter. Reading about sexual abuse and betrayal can trigger (bring on) PTSD episodes. But if you can make your way through it, good for you. We must take a hard look at the enemy if we are going to get free from it.

Pornography: Deceiver, Destroyer
Dee-Dee's story in her own words

For 34 years I was married to a porn addict. Surprisingly, I took the blame for his discontent as well as his addiction. Why? Because I loved him, trusted him, and let him define me. He implied it was my fault that his sexual needs weren't being satisfied within our marriage. And I believed him.

As a new bride, I tried meeting his needs. To put it bluntly, we had sex whenever he wanted, trying new positions, being spontaneous, every day, and sometimes more than once a day. It didn't matter if I had the flu, cramps, or an appointment; to refuse made him angry.

He told me he had a greater sexual need than other men. I believed this, too. This belief led to my sharing him with a fantasy stable of porn stars, with real women whom he engaged in emotional affairs, and even a woman with whom he had an actual affair.

Initially, I had no idea pornography was part of our marriage. But as the years passed, my husband "told" me by leaving porn around the house. When I confronted him, he told me, "Porn is something men do." Then he promised never to look at porn again. This cycle repeated three times during our marriage.

Sex was the only thing he seemed to care about, but I didn't want that to be my only value to him. I wanted to matter as a person. Yet even when we had sex, his eyes were far away, and he seemed to connect to me only physically. When he occasionally looked in my eyes, he wasn't seeing me. I felt used and heartbroken. Sex was all we had, and it was empty. I wanted our relationship to be the cake, and sex the frosting. All we had was frosting.

My husband convinced me that our marriage was bad because I couldn't give him what he wanted. Feeling like a complete failure, at times I considered suicide. So our marriage limped along until I finally admitted that we needed outside help or the marriage would end. We began Christian counseling with a psychologist whose specialty was sexual addiction.

During our first session, the psychologist told us that my husband had a pornography addiction. When I heard the official diagnosis, I was like the deer in the headlights who gets hit by the car. I was shattered. I had put my heart and soul into pleasing this man, and he had secretly cheated on me for years, looking at naked women, going into chat rooms, and who knew what else. True, he'd left samples of porn around the house, but I never suspected that they were small symbols of a huge problem. This was the moment when I realized how traumatized I had been over the years. I gave in to the trauma; I couldn't fight it anymore. I let the nightmares roll over me, the flashbacks consume me, the weight of it crush me.

We continued to go to counseling. In a later session, my husband told our psychologist that I "wasn't real" to him, and he didn't even see me as a real person. Maybe that's why every other woman in the world was more important to him. He didn't have to act like he loved me because I wasn't even there! I was trapped in a loveless marriage, had no hope that my husband would change, and was angry, sad, hurt, and disgusted all at the same time.

My husband promised a fourth time that he would never again be involved with pornography. This final promise prompted my reciprocal promise that, should he choose to return to the porn, our relationship would then be over. I refused to do this back-and-forth anymore and absolutely wouldn't participate in a fifth cycle of believing a promise only to see it broken yet again. Our psychologist asked him if I sounded serious. My husband thought so.

Except, we must remember, he didn't believe I was a real person.

Thus we began seven years of attempted recovery: education, counseling, and support groups. Eventually we would even have a two-year in-house separation to take sex out of the relationship. Due to my muddled emotional state, mental healthcare professionals recommended this action to protect me. I was literally being driven crazy over my husband's constant sexual demands and endless blaming.

Despite all these helps, however, after seven years I found him in an internet chatroom seeking sex from a total stranger. Not exactly looking at porn, but definitely following where porn leads, which is often physical unfaithfulness in the relationship. He told me he didn't think there was anything wrong with this chatroom encounter and that I just "needed to get over it."

I finally decided to file for divorce, having run out of other alternatives. In actuality, my only reason for filing was to get his attention, to end this destructive cycle of making promises and then breaking them repeatedly. I hoped he would get serious about healing if I ended this relationship he claimed meant so much to him.

But I quickly discovered this future plan wouldn't work when he asked how long it might take me to believe that he was "well." My response was, who could know? He had made it look pretty good for seven years, except for my inner misgivings. Would real healing—not simply looking like he had healed—take 10 years? 20?

As I spoke, instantly, like switching off a lamp, he dropped all civility, kindness, and reason, fully becoming the rage-filled person who usually only peeked out occasionally for a second or two. At that moment I understood what fiction authors mean by "eyes of flame" because two of them were directed at me!

Standing scant inches from my nose, he shouted, "Just remember I love you!"

Please, God, do not allow anyone else in my life to ever "love" me in that way again!

And so we went our separate ways. After more twists, turns, refusals of a just settlement, lies, "lost paperwork," and more attempted blame than in a soap opera, the divorce became final in March of 2007 Sounds like an ending, doesn't it?

The real horror story began a year later, when I was living alone. I was afraid to go to bed at night. I had no idea why, but God knew, and He took me on a seven-year journey to provide answers.

Each answer was a gentle revealing, like a flower opening, except that each petal caused another explosion in my life. It was infuriating, degrading, and beyond painful.

Ultimately, I learned that my husband, the man who had promised to love, honor, cherish, and protect me, apparently thought it his right as a super-sexed man to drug me at night (possibly with an inhalant), then sexually molest me. I had circumstantial "evidence" of his actions:

> • Since the beginning of our marriage, I had what I thought were nightmares. Looking back now, my subconscious attempt to prevent these horrors was to avoid sleeping on my back.
>
> • I woke up once in the midst of his molestation. The next day he said I'd had a nightmare. What he had done was indeed a nightmare.
>
> • After that, I started staying up ridiculously late. I didn't know why back then, but today I see that it was a subconscious way of shortening the hours my husband could have access to me.

I'm mostly healed now from those old and horrific traumas, but the fallout from his actions continues today, because my go-to-sleep time still remains unusually late.

I asked myself, *How could all this happen? How did I get such a distorted image of myself that I would stay in such a marriage?* I began looking to my childhood for answers.

I grew up a much-loved child in a good home with moral people. Then, at the tender age of seven, we visited my grandparents. I loved my grandparents' house, a real kid place: about a century old, two stories tall, and with three basements. That unmistakable scent of venerable mustiness washed over everything. Still today that odor propels me to the past and to that long-destroyed old house.

With permission to wander over the house, I went upstairs. The rooms were empty, but to my childish delight, all the doors stood open including the door to Grandpa's workshop, locked on a previous visit. Lovely furniture had come from this workshop, and now I could see where Grandpa made those things! The door was open. I went in.

A quick glance showed me that Grandpa used pictures of half-naked ladies as wallpaper! Children's brains do not have the chemical filters that adult brains do; today my adult mind recoils from this violation and my eyes would turn away, but the bright, observant child took it all in. By the time Mom flew up the stairs to determine whether "the door to Dad's workshop was closed," the damage was done. I had instantly absorbed pornography into my very being. Knowing intuitively that this wasn't a "nice" thing, I slipped into another room and told Mom that I hadn't been in the workshop, my first lie.

From that moment on, those images influenced my belief of what a woman was supposed to look like and how she should behave. Except that I never looked like one of those porn queens. But I did want to be attractive to boys. Pornography's influence, plus our culture's "disease to please," should have resulted in my developing promiscuous behavior, but they didn't. For balance there was my parents' wish that I never do anything to make them ashamed because they wanted to be proud of their daughter. I had also been "blessed" with a really delicate conscience, something at odds with growing up during the "free love" of the 1960's. I thank God for His protection!

It's odd that I was pretty, even into my 40's. Except I never realized this, always finding some imperfection in either face or figure. I could never measure up to those pictures from my childhood. Therefore, I reasoned, I must be inadequate or faulty.

Also, during my pre-teen years, my parents' business went bankrupt. My dad was so devastated that he emotionally withdrew from our family. So I became accustomed to the main man in my life—my dad—being emotionally absent. An emotionally absent man just felt "normal."

These childhood ingredients set me up for marriage failure. I unconsciously looked for a man who wasn't capable of intimacy in relationship, someone who would accept a woman with a "faulty" appearance but who might still have some value in a marriage relationship. Although I was happy to be married, feelings in my gut told me something was very wrong all those years.

But praise God the story doesn't end here! Even while I was married, God was working toward healing me. During those years:

- I learned I wasn't "crazy" when I listened to a radio call-in show hosted by two nationally known psychologists.
- I read my Bible every day.
- My Lord God cleaned out false "friends" and brought in real friends who had not only worked through their own struggles but also wanted to listen to mine. These people befriended me as I was and not as some idealized version of what they wanted me to be.

- I started attending a more caring church, where people were concerned with what was going on inside me and not just how I looked and dressed.

An introduction to Christian counseling brought more intense healing, a trickle that soon became a flood. The most important thing I learned was that I had to begin healing before I could even begin to help someone else.

Becoming emotionally healthy is an ongoing process. There's no magic formula or silver bullet.

Restarting my life was a major undertaking at age 57. However, God was and is faithful, and as soon as I accepted that he would "take care of me" (that's another story), he has completely re-made my life from the inside out.

My journey toward healing continues because I do not want the enemy of my soul, the one we call Satan, to have any kind of conquest over me. I want to be free! Most especially, I want God to be glorified in my life.

What did "becoming healthier" look like for me? My strategies for healing have included:
- Reading God's Word, the Bible, to find out who He says He is, to know what it says to do, to find out who I am, and to discover the best ways to live
- Being open to change (a scary thought!)
- Trusting my gut to tell me if something is wrong
- Seeing Godly counselors, reading Christian books, attending Life Skills and Celebrate Recovery sessions, and finding wise, mature, real friends with whom I can share openly and without fear of judgment
- Writing positive self-talk and saying it out loud as a way of rewiring misconceptions lodged in my brain
- Journaling using a computer keyboard to stimulate both sides of my brain
- Forgiving those who have hurt me (so hard to do, yet absolutely essential)

Now I'm much better than fine: I'm at peace; I'm content. In fact, call me "Victoria" because this victim has become victorious! And that is *huge*.

Advice from Dee-Dee

All of this may sound like I have this Christian life thing totally wired. Ha! I understand what to do, which is no more than the old hymn "Trust and Obey" says.

Lots of times, however, I'm not "be(ing) still and know(ing) that He is God." (Psalm 46:10) Or I may be running ahead like Jonah, or jumping to conclusions like Peter, or doing what I think God wants like Saul, when actually I'm not following His words and am making it up as I go along. Disastrous. Always.

I've learned that God is good! Trust Him as though your life depends on it, because it does.

God bless you! Let go of the pain. Let God begin the healing.

***

Insights from Dee-Dee's Story
Forgiveness

It can seem impossible to forgive another person who has done such damage to your life, yet Dee-Dee managed to forgive. Forgiveness is essential to healing; without it, you allow the other person to have power over you through ongoing resentment, negative memories, and other influences that prevent you from healing. If you're struggling with forgiveness, read on for some helpful strategies.

First, forgiveness *does not mean* you have to:
- Let the other person off the hook, believing the perpetrator should not have to face the consequences
- Trust the other person
- Deny that it really happened
- Forget that it happened

Forgiveness is something we do because God forgave us and because it's necessary for *our own* healing. The act of forgiveness:

- Frees us from emotional prison
- Helps us let go of bitterness and move on with our lives
- Is a decision, not a feeling
- Can be a process instead of a one-time, clear-the-slate act
- Is, no matter what, difficult to do in situations involving trauma

The bottom line: If you can find the compassion to forgive someone who has grievously hurt you, you have the power to transform your own reality by putting the incident in the past and setting yourself free. As author Linda Graham[1] says:

> Forgiveness does not mean condoning, pardoning, forgetting, false reconciliation, appeasement, or sentimentality.... It is a practice ... that allows us to ... reset our moral compass, and to remain compassionate even in the face of injustice, betrayal, and harm.

More about forgiveness

Meditation is another way to get to the point of forgiveness. Here's a meditation example you might try saying to yourself about the person you've decided to forgive:

> *I remember the many ways you have hurt, wounded, or harmed me—out of fear, pain, confusion, or anger. I have carried this pain in my heart long enough. To the extent that I am ready, I offer you forgiveness. To you who has caused me harm, I offer my forgiveness. I forgive you.*

About sexual/porn addiction

By discussing pornography and sexual addiction here, there is no intention of pointing fingers, seeing the problem as black or white, or condemning a person who is having difficulty with pornography and addiction. As much as anyone with PTSD, sexual/porn addicts are trapped, usually want a way out, and would give anything to heal those who have been hurt. If this sounds like you, please don't condemn yourself; but please do seek professional help, be honest with those you're accountable to, and aim for recovery.

Why pornography is so dangerous
If a person views porn repeatedly, the brain will literally rewire itself. Looking at an erotic image for mere tenths of a second triggers your brain to pump out chemicals and form new nerve pathways, leading to profound and lasting changes. Hardly anything can compete with porn for your attention, including having actual sex with a real partner. How can that be? Porn creates the perfect conditions and triggers the release of the right chemicals for maximum pleasure—and makes lasting changes in your brain.

Your brain drives behavior, so a porn-saturated brain is very likely to lead you to act out in ways that are unhealthy and even illegal.

Other adverse effects of pornography use include:
- The abuse and mistreatment of individuals involved in filming porn, putting them at risk of sexually transmitted diseases, abusing alcohol and drugs, and committing violence
- Increasingly hostile and demeaning views of women among users
- Increasing opinions and treatment of women as sex objects
- Early availability of porn to children via home computers
- Film content containing violence, degradation, and humiliation of women

Why sexual addiction is so difficult to overcome

All addictions pose daunting challenges to their victims. But sexual addition is different in at least one significant way: It's almost impossible to avoid temptation. Alcoholics, for example, can avoid temptation by refusing to hang out with their former drinking buddies, avoiding bars, and clearing all the alcohol out of their homes; and it's still extremely tough for them to conquer the habit.

But sexual addicts can't pull away from the everyday world full of attractive women wherever they look, and they can't destroy the mental images they've permanently filed in their brains, so sexual temptations are always with them, inside and out. Accountability groups, sexual addiction counseling, and computer monitoring are all essential strategies for recovery—and reasons to hope that recovery will last, marriages will be saved, and families will be healed.

Life Skills and Celebrate Recovery

These two programs, mentioned in Dee-Dee's story, offer biblically based classes in recovery from addictions and past hurts, and in developing character traits for a better future. If you're interested, check to see if these or similar programs are offered in your area. Classes like these are powerful ways to begin healing from PTSD, pornography addiction, or other life challenges you've encountered. See the resources section in the back of this book for more information.

The trauma of betrayal and abuse

When people pledge their wedding vows or otherwise commit to each other in a relationship, they expect their partner, among other things, to be faithful in thought, word, and deed. Yet tens of thousands of people are betrayed by their partners every day. These betrayals feel like nothing less than a knife to the heart for those who still love their unfaithful partners.

The shock of discovery can be so profound that faithful partners become traumatized and often develop PTSD. When partners look intently or multiple times at other women or other men, or if they actually have physical contact with these outsiders, their actions often sound the death knell of a marriage or a committed relationship. Jesus himself spells out the basics of adultery in Matthew 5:27-28:

> You know the next commandment pretty well, too: 'Don't go to bed with another's spouse.' But don't think you've preserved your virtue simply by staying out of bed. Your heart can be corrupted by lust even quicker than your body. Those leering looks you think nobody notices— they also corrupt.

An Unexpected Deliverance
In Sylvie's words

It was another dark, cold winter night in the little house in my new hometown. I was so sad and lonely I didn't know how I was going to survive the few hours until bedtime. So I flopped onto my couch and began my nightly ritual. Google *PTSD*. Google *trauma*. Look for some new twist on how to break free from these vicious captors. Look for new medications. Look for anything that would put my shattered self back together, that would stop the invasive flashbacks that constantly filled my mind. I closed my eyes and thought back over the past five years.

Five years ago in another city, I married Mark, the love of my life. We had a fairy-tale marriage for seven months ... until I saw my beloved betray me, right before my eyes. That Sunday, I sat in church watching my handsome husband onstage with the worship band. Mark flashed his eyes and put on a sexy smile. I thought he was looking at me. But no. His target was another woman who was momentarily next to me as she walked down the side aisle to the front row.

He continued to make eyes at the slim, blonde woman while he played his guitar. *I'm right here!*, I wanted to shout. *How could he do such a thing, especially in front of me—and in church?* In the span of two or three songs, Mark wiped out our past, our present, and my future. He brazenly destroyed my world and traumatized me.

Later on that shocking Sunday, Mark disclosed that he had been viewing pornography since the age of 17. The man I thought I married didn't exist. Years earlier when I was 16, my own father's betrayal had devastated my mother. I promised

45

myself then never to marry a betrayer. It was too late. I had made that fatal mistake, and I crumbled like a crushed clay pot.

And it got worse. Even though Mark may have eventually stopped viewing pornography, years of engaging in this sexual addiction had hard-wired his brain. He couldn't—or wouldn't—stop looking multiple times at attractive women while standing right next to me, He drove us on odd routes so he could travel streets frequented by girls and women in bikinis and jogging shorts. He carried on flirtatious, intimate conversations with other women at parties. At Disneyland, Mark once told a young teenage girl who was wearing short shorts that he was getting "excited." Each instance left me sick to my stomach for weeks, and the scenes replayed themselves in my head every waking moment. PTSD was setting up camp inside me as the traumas kept coming.

What PTSD was like for me:

- My entire reality shattered when Mark locked his eyes, long and lasciviously, on another woman who passed right next to me and sat a mere three rows away in church. It was like watching him have sex with another woman. Suddenly I was spinning in a scary new world that had careened out of control.
- I couldn't get away—I was trapped in my pew. I was also trapped in a marriage to a man who read his Bible, participated in church leadership, and prayed for others, but who somehow couldn't see his straying eyes as sinful behavior.
- The shock in my marriage awakened earlier traumas in my life. Molestation as an infant by my father and, later, his raging, drinking, and womanizing rose from my deadened memories to haunt me.
- I would start to trust again. Then Mark would betray me, looking repeatedly at women who crossed his path or turning away from me in a restaurant to ogle an

especially lovely pair of legs. Once Mark literally waltzed into our kitchen to greet one of my guests, dressed only in a T-shirt and sleeping shorts that weren't long enough to cover everything. Going out into the world with my husband was fraught with potential trauma, and now trauma had struck at home.

- After acting out, Mark usually denied his errant behavior. Then, "Well, maybe I did do it but I didn't intend to." This cycle repeated endlessly, and Mark began to make me out as the bad wife "who gets upset over nothing." In truth, I was a wife who was always upset. I couldn't get control of PTSD or myself.
- I constantly relived the traumatic incidents as if they were happening in real time. My heart pounded. I had nightmares. I had to quit my job. I obsessively worked on arts and crafts. My hands had to be busy from morning until late at night. I dreaded going to bed and awoke at three or four a.m. every day, electrified with anxiety. My self-confidence deserted me in a world full of women that Mark found more attractive and desirable than his own wife.
- I lost my sense of who I was and became a frenzied, unstable person who was barely surviving. I was taking so much medicine to keep deeper depression and suicidal thoughts at bay that I walked, talked, and acted like someone I'd never known. My world, my very self, had been obliterated. I wasn't "me" for five long years. PTSD kept playing the shocking images and movies in my mind, and I relived them over and over.

I soon didn't just have PTSD. I *was* PTSD. It took over my life. But I still loved my husband and didn't want to lose my marriage, so I went to Cognitive Behavioral Therapy for a year and a half. Finally my counselor said, "You have to leave your husband. He's just going to keep hurting you." Yet I stayed. And the cycle of betrayals continued through three years of marriage counseling. By that time, I was hyper-vigilant, worried, afraid, ruminating obsessively on each incident, living in a shocking world where life seemed unendurable.

One agonizing night as I lay sobbing in bed, I heard a voice. I really did. "I have other things for you to do," the Lord said lovingly to me. Finally I decided I had to move away to save what was left of myself. It was a wrenching decision. I still loved the man I thought I married. But staying with Mark those five years had profoundly damaged both my mental and physical health. I moved 1800 miles from my beautiful lakeside hometown, where I'd lived for over 40 years, to the Northeast, where I now live near my daughters and grandchildren.

That was just the beginning of PTSD's second onslaught on my mind, body, spirit, and soul.

When I arrived in my new hometown, I quickly joined an evangelical church. I went forward for prayer the first Sunday I attended, sobbing uncontrollably. Later, one of the church leaders told me, "You were just raw emotion. We had never seen anything like it."

But God had me where he wanted me—in a loving, caring church whose members would help me heal. Solidly planted in a caring church, I next identified community resources that could also help me. Psychiatrist. Christian counselor. Phone-in therapy groups for wives of men addicted to porn/sex. I added EMDR (Eye Movement Desensitization and Reprocessing), a leading treatment for people with PTSD.

Even after 13 months of hard work in my new home, I wasn't getting better. I kept reading that most people have PTSD for the rest of their lives. That sounded like a death sentence. I decided that somehow I was going to take control of it.

By that time, I had developed a visualization of PTSD, trauma, and molestation as evils that had invaded my life. I wanted those evils *out*. As I lay on the couch that January night, searching online for cures, I recalled a type of prayer with "laying on of hands." I thought, *That's one thing I haven't tried.*

I sent an email to the elder of prayer at my new church, briefly describing the problem and asking if laying-on-of-hands prayer was available to me. He wrote back that it was available and soundly endorsed by the pastors. Then he added, "I believe that you also need the ministry of deliverance." What was that? I soon found out.

I received a book to read, *The Power of Deliverance,* by author Bill Banks. As I suspected, it talked about expelling demons from one's life. That sounded a little extreme, a little wacko, a little frightening. But after all, I thought, I had indeed identified specific evils that were within me. The New Testament was full of stories of Jesus casting out demons. Maybe this was how I could get the evil out and maybe, just maybe, break free of PTSD. So I agreed to try deliverance prayer.

The first step in the process was writing names of anyone I needed to forgive. Then I wrote about the sins in my own life that I hadn't confessed. After that, I made a list of the bothersome "troubles" (often called "entities") inside me. Now I was ready to meet with my deliverance team and take the plunge.

The elder of prayer, his wife (who is gifted in prayer), and the Minister of Community Care sat with me in a cozy room with lots of light and a crackling fire.

First we talked about forgiving Mark. I reasoned that people who have addictions have almost always experienced some kind of trauma themselves. Of course I could forgive a man whose "child inside" had been deeply hurt. I knew what that could be like. I forgave Mark.

Next, my father. Years earlier I learned that he had molested my sister, but at that time I didn't know if I'd also been a victim. I thought it likely, though. So back then, I gave him "pre-forgiveness." I decided that if someday I found out that he'd hurt me, I would forgive him. My father had a traumatic childhood and was further traumatized while fighting during World War II. That pre-forgiveness had allowed me to care for my father through the end of his life.

I confessed a serious sin I had committed years ago. I asked God to forgive me. I thought about actions I had taken that I still felt guilty about. So I asked God to help me forgive my own sins, as He already had.

Together, my prayer team and I named and listed on paper the evil spirits that had moved into my life: betrayal, bitterness, a continued unhealthy bond with my ex-husband, trauma, PTSD, depression, poor self-image, anger, resentment, control, abandonment, and more. The preparations were complete; I was ready to pray.

The prayer warriors came around me, put their hands on my head and shoulders, and began praying in Jesus' name for these evils to leave, one at a time. I repeated their prayers and began to feel a churning inside me.

I actually felt the evils leave me. Some just slipped away. Others were stubborn, and I mentally ripped them out from where they were embedded in me.

We prayed through the entire list, then ended the prayer. It was a little like waking from a dream. I couldn't define my feelings. The elder asked me to put the list of evils into the fireplace, where it burned away. When I turned around from the fire, he said my countenance had changed.

I realized that I felt peaceful and free. I walked out to the car, light on my feet and grinning. I felt so clean.

I treasured this time of newness, this experience of God loving me and the Holy Spirit filling me. I was no longer lonely! I no longer resented Mark! For possibly the first time in my life I experienced deep peace.

The next morning I expected to wake up with a sense of dread, as I had every previous day of my life. But no—I was smiling! I could connect to God! The dark mass between me and my Maker was gone, and I could hear His voice, feel Him reaching to me. I could trust Him completely with my future—whatever He wanted really was the best for me. I believed it. I was content.

Now I stand guard against the evils day and night. Luke 11:24 explains that when God expels an evil spirit, it hangs around. If its previous "home" (host, or person) stays empty, the evil spirit returns with even more demons, and they move back into the delivered person's life. The person plunges into suffering that is much worse than before.

When I forget to be watchful, or when a nightmare sneaks up on me, my heart still races, and I panic from fear. During my conscious hours, I hold PTSD at bay with these strategies:

- Fill my empty "house" with the Holy Spirit
- Praise and thank God that I've tasted freedom
- Read and study the Bible, trying to live by its guidelines
- Maintain close contact with other Christians who can encourage me and hold me accountable
- Engage in activities that give me a sense of purpose and meaning

I'm a new woman now, building a new life. Imagine breaking free from an alligator that's been savaging you, threatening your very existence. I survived my battle with that alligator, PTSD, for five years. The beast has let go of me and crawled into deeper, darker waters. But it left me with some parts missing and others in shreds. I need time to heal and build a new life. That alligator is still in my pond; once in a while it rakes me with its scaly hide. PTSD is not completely wiped from my life, but I have much better control over it now.

Advice from Sylvie

If you have PTSD, grit your teeth and take back your life! Open your heart to God. Read everything you can find, get good counsel, get medication if you need it (I did), shout down flashbacks, join support groups, talk about it. Take good care of yourself, exercise, make friends, have some fun. Boldly stand against evil! Your Father is the King of the Universe! His Angel Armies are on your side.

***

Insights from Sylvie's Story
Husbands looking at other women

People are programmed to appreciate beauty. To most men, women are beautiful. But some men, especially those addicted to porn, look again or multiple times, look longer, and greedily soak in everything they can with each penetrating glance.

Jesus says, "But I tell you that anyone who looks at a woman lustfully has already committed adultery with her in his heart." (Matthew 5:28). When wives see their husbands looking this way at pornography or other women, they feel betrayed; their wedding vows have been violated. These women can become shattered and traumatized, as Sylvie was.

Hearing the voice of God

You may be having a hard time believing that Sylvie really heard God's voice in the night and saw the image of pornography and molestation as a "black bag of evil." Others of you readily believe this, perhaps because you've experienced something similar yourself. The Bible speaks of many individuals who heard God's voice: Samuel, Elijah, Jonah, Saul/Paul, the disciples of Jesus, to name a few. This phenomenon occurs especially to people who have certain spiritual gifts, but it can and does happen to many other Christ-followers regardless of their gifts.

Because this divine communication can manifest in many forms, you can take specific actions if you want to hear God's voice, including:

- Read your Bible regularly and apply its teachings to your life
- Be a good listener to people and to God
- Practice patience; wait on God
- Build your awareness of God's presence in your life
- Obey God and grow steadily closer to Him
- Look for God at work in your life

Ultimately, though, it's God who determines which individuals need specific direction from Him.

Cognitive Behavioral Therapy (CBT)

CBT is a psychotherapy that helps people change unhelpful thinking and behavior into more objective and analytical ideas, helping improve their mood and ability to function day-to-day. For example, Sylvie's CBT counselor asked her to look at a trauma or problem in a variety of ways and to challenge her thinking about the issue. She asked herself questions such as: Do other people see the problem the way I see it? Do I have facts that support my view of the problem? What are other ways I could view the problem? By answering these questions, she was able to see the problem and possible solutions from a variety of perspectives and more objectively.

Eye Movement Desensitization and Reprocessing (EMDR)

EMDR is a psychotherapy treatment that was originally designed to alleviate the distress associated with traumatic memories. During Sylvie's sessions, she focused on troubling memories and described them aloud while her therapist rhythmically tapped Sylvie's knees, back and forth, during the telling. The taps crossed the midline of Sylvie's body and helped the logical side of her brain process the memory, adding objectivity to her already racing emotions. After a session, Sylvie was better able to realize that the event was something that had happened in the past and that she could now let it go and move on. This therapy can also reduce flashbacks and obsessive or intrusive thoughts.

Importance of a support network

If you have PTSD and don't already have a support network of family or friends, you can build a support team by sharing your story with friends, counselors, clergy, or family members who are wise and discerning and can also be trusted. If these people are "safe" (confidential, empathetic), they will listen to you as you share your story again and again (once just doesn't provide the relief you need). They cheer your progress and empathize when you're "stuck." They truly want to see you succeed in managing PTSD and building your new life.

Pornography and the church

Current statistics[1] cite that 65-70% of Christian men view porn. One has only to talk with pastors, lay ministers, and counselors of Christians to have these statistics validated anecdotally. Pornography is one of the biggest—and most secret—problems in the church today.

Your Story
When, Where, Why It Happened

As you continue to put words to your story, it will help to describe the setting, grounding it in reality. It will help you realize that the event happened in the past, and that it was real. It may assure you that the past is now over. The trauma isn't still happening. But the details you add will give solidity to your story. Your story is true.

First step

Answer some or all the following questions:

- Where were you?
- What kind of place was it?
- Who else was there?
- What kind of day was it?
- What time of day did it take place?

Include the details of the incident as well as your sensory experience: What did you touch, what happened to your body (heart rate, breathing), how long did the experience take, what colors, noises, odors do you remember?

Example

Sylvie might have answered the questions above like this:

- **Where were you?** In church, third row from the front, on the right-side aisle
- **What kind of place was it?** Bright, filled with music and worship
- **Who else was there?** About 100 people in the congregation, with friends sitting nearby
- **What kind of day was it?** Sunny, warm, beautiful fall day

• **What time of day did it take place?** Just as the 9 a.m. service was beginning

Second step
Flesh out your story with answers to the questions above and other details and sensory experiences you can remember.

Example
For example, Sylvie might have written:
"The worship music at the start of the service was my favorite part, especially because my husband of seven months was playing in the band. I was so proud of him. I sang and clapped with the other worshippers, about 100 of them. The doors stood open and the fresh fall breeze wafted into the sanctuary, the morning sun sparkling against the stained-glass windows, almost bringing them to life …" (this story would go on to describe the "where" of the entire incident)

Take a few moments to write your version.

_____

_____

_____

_____

_____

_____

_____

Section C
Trauma and PTSD from Domestic Abuse

Natalie was sore and heartsick. She'd caught a glimpse of her face in the mirror, and the sight was horrifying. With black eyes and a swollen nose, she couldn't leave the house anyway so she climbed back in bed. Natalie had moved in with Marco just a week ago, and he'd never been anything but kind and loving. But last night he came home drunk and beat her to a pulp. Her head hurt, her ribs ached, and she noticed a pinkish tinge to her urine. She had to think of something before Marco returned! Problem was, she couldn't leave or she'd be homeless again. Maybe this was better than being homeless.

If you see yourself in any part of this tragic story, I'm so sorry for your circumstances and the damage being done to you. We may not know each other, but I'd like to arm you with some information because I want you to be safe.

If some items in the lists below sound familiar to you, it doesn't necessarily mean that you're in an abusive situation. But it may mean that it's a good idea to pay close attention to your situation to keep it from escalating. My heart is with you, and you can respond directly at my website, which you'll find at the back of this book.

Here we go.

Some types of domestic abuse
Domestic abuse is any behavior that aims at gaining or maintaining power and control over another person in the household. These are types of domestic abuse:
1. Emotional abuse, rejection, ignoring, terrorizing
2. Isolation, imprisonment
3. Minimizing, denying, and blaming
4. Intimidation, threats, deriding, name-calling, humiliation

5. Using money to demean or control
6. Spiritual abuse, use of Scripture to control, use of "submission" to force unwanted acts
7. Using words that are degrading, demeaning, or insulting

Domestic violence

Domestic abuse is about power. Domestic abuse often escalates to domestic violence, which includes sexual molestation, rape, hitting, kicking, punching, burning, and more. Natalie's abuse probably falls into both categories.

Everyone deserves to be safe

Thousands of men, women, and children are abused every day in living situations that God meant to be safe for us: homes, schools, community groups. Are you in such a situation? To help decide, check the following lists for feelings or facts that seem familiar to you. If you find some items that apply to you, you're not alone. Most people experience one or more of these feelings at some point in life. Many resources (in the Resource section of this book) exist to help you get to a safe place.

Do you:
- Feel afraid of your partner much of the time?
- Avoid certain topics out of fear of angering your partner?
- Feel that you can't do anything right for your partner?
- Believe that you deserve to be hurt or mistreated?
- Wonder if you're the one who is crazy?
- Feel emotionally numb or helpless?

Does the other person:
- Humiliate, yell, blame, or criticize you?
- Ignore or put down your ideas or accomplishments?
- See you as a sex object, not as a person?
- Have a bad temper, hurt you, threaten to kill you?
- Threaten suicide if you leave?

- Destroy your belongings?
- Become jealous, keep you from seeing friends or family?
- Limit how much money you can have?
- Check up on you constantly?

If this is happening to you, or to someone you know, I want to commend you on your courage to acknowledge this truth. You and I both wish you weren't in such a situation. You may not see a way out right now, but you can take steps to protect yourself. Consider calling a hotline, going to a safe house, talking with a counselor, or telling a parent, teacher, pastor, or priest.

You have eternal value and deserve to be and feel safe.

Why Do Your Face Glow?
Maya, in her own words

It's been very difficult for me, you know. I was born in Birmingham, Alabama. My father took me away from my mother at a young age cause she was an alcoholic. He took me and my brother to live with Aunt Bertha. She was a beautiful lady, very smart. She had plenty of money because she kept mentally ill people in her house and also worked in the kitchen of a luxury hotel.

But she put my brother and me in the cellar. We lived down there, on a dirt floor and with dirt walls. No heat, either. Our beds was old clothes that had been donated for the mentally ill residents. I did get to come up in the daytime. That's when I washed pots and pans for Aunt Bertha or sometimes went to school. In school, they made me sit out in the hall cause I smelled so bad.

After a long time, my father came to get my brother and me to live with him and his new wife. One thing that has happened to me all my life (my dad having sexual relations with me) got worse when I moved into his house. Pretty soon it was other older men that my sister's friends let him do to me. And then my step-brothers. This was happening with my sisters too.

When I was 16, my father sent me to Memphis, Tennessee. I was one of 12 children, but I was the only one my father sent away. I've been on my own ever since.

I asked God why my father sent me here and separated me from everything, and why I got depression and PTSD. And I believe the Lord told me it was because my dad didn't want to father a child with me.

On my own in Memphis, I was making the wrong choices in boyfriends, in husbands, you know—looking for someone who was like my dad, but who would love me. You marry somebody and you share things with them and you think their heart is going to go out for you, but it's turned around. And whenever there was an argument, they do what your dad did.

I have children. I couldn't see them when I was such a mess. I can see them now. I also have three deceased kids, one where my husband suffocated and killed my baby, and I miscarried twins.

I got real angry with God, you know. I said "You knew me before I came into the world, so why did you let all this happen to me? Sleeping in my car, shelter to shelter, bed bugs, you know, the whole thing. I was with this man and that man because that was the way I was brought up.

I actually wanted to die like my mom died, cirrhosis at age 58. I was drinking to die. My mom, you know, she was an alcoholic. So I was born with Alcohol Syndrome. And I drank. I couldn't get an answer from God because I was just drinking and had it my way. I drank and drank for years. And it broke my family up. I couldn't see my grandbabies because I was drinking. I think I stayed at just about all the shelters in Memphis. The reason being that I'd come in drunk, and I'd have to leave. And I understand that.

Well, there came a time when I got really bad, and I tried to kill my son. So he called the paramedics, and I got put in the psych ward. I got a psychiatrist, and he worked on my chemical imbalance for depression and PTSD. I do take antidepressants now, and I have to take sleep medicine because I can't sleep. I saw my psychiatrist starting 15 years ago. I talked to him about my dad.

My psychiatrist said, "Maya, the only way you're gonna rid that is to face your enemy. Is your father living? You need to go to him personally and let him know what he's done to you."

So I was in my fifties on my journey to Alabama. I went to my dad's house and said my prayer, "Lord, please protect me from the enemy." I went in and let my dad know I wanted to talk about this. He just abruptly jumped up and pulled out a knife. My sister ran one way and I ran the other way. So then I left and went back to my sister's house.

But I was just so tired of having these dreams as I got older and older. I prayed and said, "Lord, I know you sent me here, through my psychiatrist, so I could rid this." So I went back to my dad's the next day, and when I saw him, I said, "I'm here again cause I need to go back to Memphis with my family. And he couldn't move! It was so amazing to me that I just started talking. "Dad, why did you do this to me? What did I do wrong? I'm sorry for whatever I did wrong. Why did you do this to me?"

He said, "You just lyin' and lyin'."

I told him "I love you dearly because I have to, but I hate what you brought into my life. I'm on medication, I have no more husband." (I'd been married two or three times at that time.) I said, "You know, every figure was a figure of you."

Here I am. I'm 62. I was homeless for 6 years. And I thought, *What the heck is going on with God? Where are you? What have I done to go through all this?*

So I went from shelter to shelter, but kept praying, "Lord, if I could just have a place to call my own, I'd be more comfortable, and I could be myself."

A friend came to see me and told me she was going to help me get an apartment, but she said there was no alcohol allowed in it. In that moment it seemed like I heard God whisper, "I delivered you." And after that I never had a taste, or desire, for alcohol again. It was really phenomenal to me.

It's been going on five years now, no drinking. I am so thankful. You know every day is a new day, a new beginning in my life to get myself together.

So this is crazy. My friend *did* get me an apartment! I don't understand this. I never had anyone to love me. And when they came into my apartment, WOW! They came with couches, beds, and tables, and I didn't have nothing but the clothes on my back. I just started to cry. When they blessed me with a home, you could have bought me with a penny! I just couldn't believe it.

My friend saw something in me. And now she's my accountant, which means she pays my bills and gives me an allowance. In my first week, I ran out of cigarettes. She said, "Sorry! You don't get your next money until Sunday." Nobody ever taught that to me. So now I know how to budget. "Do you want to smoke?" she asked. "Then save your money. I don't want to have no argument about money between us."

God wants me to talk with shelter ladies. This is what he wants me to do. I have faith but I still have so many gloomy days you know, so that's why I try to keep myself busy. Oh I can help somebody and then go home, and that's a good feeling. But don't let me sit at home because I can't contain things.

I was so glad when He blessed me with a car, you know, because I was going here and there on bus to bus to bus.

I always wanted to be a mentor to ladies who have gone through so much because I've been through so much. I love seeing God work because everybody has to experience Him in their own way. So when this new shelter opens, I'll have that opportunity again. And that's good for me. But I don't know; I'm just so lonely and I'm feeling like dang, what am I doing here? I don't have a husband, I got no pet, and I have a roommate who is talking about moving out.

When I talk with some people they say, "How in the world are you living?" I say, "By the grace of God." I wake up in the morning and try to read a little in the Word, meditate and pray a little bit, and get up and get about my day.

Somebody said, "Maya, why do your face glow?" I said, "Ask me about what's inside of me!" So I give Him thanks.

When people start loving on me, it feels good! I can't believe it. And then I can pass that on.

Now it seems like I'm not doing enough for the Lord. I ask, "What else you want me to do? I don't feel like I'm doing enough. I'm going to find a purpose."

I do believe I will because of a dream back 22 years. I was depressed. And somebody came to me in the dream and took me to this big tent. She said these are the people you have to take care of! And that was 22 years ago. And now I'm going to do it. So I guess I don't have to ask "What's my purpose?" anymore.

One woman told me, "You don't look like you been in a shelter." And I say to her, "After I tell you my story, you're gonna be on your feet just like me." I think that's really what they need. An example. Somebody who gets it.

Advice from Maya
What I would really like is, if you can find yourself in my story, to know that you too can be healed from these things we suffer with. My feeling is that when we don't open up, we bury things. And when we open up we bloom like a flower.

Seeking that special person to talk to is so important because they have a heart and have experienced some things like you have. I said, "Why me, why me, why me?" He said, "Why *not* you? I cry when you cry, and I hurt when you hurt. I'm shaping and molding you in the image I have for you." I learned to take the punches because God took them first for us. Just keep falling down and getting back up.

***

Insights from Maya's story
Domestic abuse/violence
If you look back at the introduction to this section, you'll see that the information pointed directly to the many types of abuse Maya experienced in her life. The abuse began when she was a baby and continued into adulthood. That she survived this and is

thriving even as I write her story today makes her story all the more amazing.

Do you know or pass by people like Maya? After I heard her story (and believe me, there's much more to it), I saw her in a different light. She changed the way I think about people who are homeless and struggling for their very lives. All these people have stories. They were little children once, they want to be loved, and they deserve our respect.

One way to start a conversation with a homeless person is to ask, "What happened to you? What is your story?" You might be surprised at what you hear, and you'll surely be changed. Perhaps being listened to will change the other person's life too.

Childhood assaults

Child abusers often think, "The child won't remember this, so it's okay." But children do remember and carry the hurt into their adult lives. Trauma expert Bessel A. van der Kolk[1] makes this dramatic point:

> Eradicating child abuse in America would reduce
> the overall rate of depression by more than half,
> alcoholism by two-thirds, and suicide, IV drug
> use, and domestic violence by three-quarters.

Sexual abuse is a particularly heinous type of child abuse. Most readers are appalled when they hear about the sexual trauma Maya endured at the hands of her father—who was supposed to protect and nurture her. And it is appalling, especially that she was handed around from infancy until she was 16 to brothers, step-brothers, and various other men.

When things like this happen to children, they have no way to process it except to be in constant fear: fear of pain, fear of humiliation, fear of death. Since this was the family system Maya's father set up, even her step-mother knew what was going on and didn't say or do anything about the abuse. Esteemed author and expert on abuse, Diane Langberg[2] says:

The sexual abuse of a child shatters and violates every aspect of their being—their world, their self, their faith, and their future... Such violation causes the child to develop a view of himself and his world that is based on repeated lies, evil, and destruction.

Maya's adult body gave her the first alert that something terrible had happened in the past. Of course, she remembered some things but had repressed many more. The horrifying nightmares that boiled up carried messages for her about her past. Sudden pain in private parts of her body told Maya where and what type of sexual attacks had occurred. These "body memories" forced her to experience the pain and fear all over again.

Trauma expert Bessel A. van der Kolk[3] agrees with Maya's psychiatrist about how she must resolve her past so she can put it away:

As long as you keep secrets and suppress information, you are fundamentally at war with yourself....The critical issue is allowing yourself to know what you know. That takes an enormous amount of courage.

Figures and shadows

Maya told her father that "Every figure was a figure of you." She explains that the husbands and boyfriends she chose always turned out to be like her father in some way: abusive, demeaning, and terrorizing. They were "figures" of her father.

Figure is a literary term that draws similarities between characters. For example, in Psalms, a book of the Bible, David was a figure of Christ because he shared many of Jesus' characteristics, such as passion, strength, courage in the face of adversity, and his deeply devoted reverence of God.

But, as with most things, there can be a dark parallel when it comes to figures, which was what Maya experienced.

Nightmares, dreams, and more

Nightmares and dreams at night. Body memories upon waking or falling to sleep. Flashbacks. All these occurrences keep past trauma alive for months or years after the event. Trauma nightmares usually include elements of the actual trauma, forcing the victim to relive the experience over and over again—as if it were in real time, heart pounding, panicky breathing. People who have PTSD, however, are more likely to dream exact replays. I know what this is like, and if you have experienced it too, my heart goes out to you.

These nightmares are more likely to occur earlier in the night and during different stages of sleep. They also often cause body movements (thrashing, stiffening, sitting up, crying out) to occur during the dreams.

Several treatments have been developed for those who experience these alarming events:

- Imagery Rehearsal Therapy (IRT) helps the patient, while awake, give the nightmare a new ending that is not scary. Then the person replays in his/her mind the new dream many times.
- Improving nighttime breathing can help prevent or reduce violent, scary dreams.
- Prazosin is a medication that can help reduce nightmares and improve overall functioning for people with PTSD.

Maya's dreams included elements like these:

- Her father chasing after her, yelling, "Come on! It's your time!"
- Her Aunt Bertha chasing her with huge pots and pans that needed to be scrubbed, with many more piles of pans stacked around the kitchen

- Her father coming after her with a gun, trying to shoot her

Complex trauma

In recent years, mental health practitioners have identified another type of PTSD: Complex Post-Traumatic Stress Disorder, or C-PTSD. In her book *The Complex PTSD Workbook*, author Arielle Schwartz, Ph.D[4], describes C-PTSD as typically arising "as a result of ongoing stress or repeated traumatic events that occur during childhood." She includes this list of experiences that can result in C-PTSD:

- Childhood relationships with parents or caregivers that are frightening, unpredictable, and/or overwhelming
- Ongoing or repeated experiences of neglect or physical, verbal, or sexual abuse
- Growing up with exposure to domestic violence
- Being raised by a caregiver who has an active addiction or untreated mental illness
- Experiencing abuse at especially vulnerable times of development, such as early childhood or adolescence
- Facing severe social stress such as bullying, disability, or exposure to traumatic events within your community without support by a caregiver who protects and cares for you
- Being discriminated against or feeling disempowered without a caregiver who helps advocate for you or takes responsibility for your needs

As of this writing, C-PTSD is not included in the Diagnostic and Statistical Manual of Mental Disorders (DSM) 5. But when you look at the many types of abuse and the lengthy periods of time that Maya endured abuse, surely she would have qualified for this designation of C-PTSD. It's amazing to me that she persisted in living, and even more amazing that she's finally realizing some of her dreams from years ago.

How do you relate to homeless people?

If you've been touched by Maya's story (as I was), I hope you'll consider how to interact with the downtrodden, abused, and homeless people you encounter. Can you see them, make eye contact, say hello? Any simple gesture like this acknowledges their humanity. Are you prepared for people on the streets who ask for handouts? Perhaps we could all stop and say, "What are some things you need? What could I get for you?" A simple bottle of water or a warm scarf to protect from the cold can change a person's day, just because they're treated like real people. Getting involved with shelters and organizations that aid homeless people is another option.

To be honest, this is a difficult subject for me. I've paid for a meal for a man, offered to buy groceries for a woman and her child, and even arranged temporary housing for a homeless family. But it wasn't easy, and sometimes it wasn't what they really wanted. But passing them by like they're invisible doesn't seem like a good option to me anymore. These are the ones Jesus called us to minister to. I hope we can continue this discussion on my website, sydneysegen.com, or on one of my Facebook pages, "Hope after Trauma and PTSD" and "Stories of Trauma, PTSD, and Hope."

Now that we know Maya's story, we can better understand what brings many abused and homeless people to their situations. Often, homeless people suffer from trauma and PTSD with no hope on the horizon. As we grow in our ability to hope, perhaps we can extend hope to others.

Your Story
This Is How It Feels to Me

Now that you've completed "what happened to you" and added details to put your story in real time, we're ready to take a look at adding emotion to your story. This step may be difficult because you will have to look back at how the incident made you feel, but if you can muscle through this section, you will have captured the heart of your story ... because you put your heart into it.

First step
Answer some or all the following questions:

> • What are some of the positive feelings you remember? If you don't have any of these, don't be concerned. After all, we're writing about something difficult that occurred in your life.
> • What feelings of shock or trauma do you remember? How did you react (body and emotions) to the shock at the time? How have your feelings of shock changed over time?
> • What are some negative emotions you felt during or after the incident?

Example
Maya might have answered the questions above like this:

> • **What are some of the positive feelings you remember?** Hope when I got a new start; blessed numbness when I passed out from drinking; fear when I confronted my father; joy when my friend stepped up to help me get an apartment; thrilled

when I saw my new furniture; gratitude when I finally got a job
- **What feelings of shock or trauma do you remember?** I thought moving to my aunt's house would be better for me, but I was in for a shock; when my father started passing me around to other men, I felt terror; when I was on the streets, I was desperate; today I still sometimes have those feelings, along with fear
- **What are some negative emotions you felt during or after the incident?** Fear; unclean; un-cared-for; ashamed; worthless; hopeless; like I wanted to die

Second step
Flesh out your story with answers to the questions above and other details and emotions you can remember.

Example
For example, Maya might have written:
"When I got to Memphis, all alone at age 16, I was scared out of my wits. I had no money, didn't know anyone, and felt like I wanted to give up. Then I met some people on the street, and they showed me how I could get by. I was so grateful for that. One of the people had an apartment and asked me to move in. At first I was elated. I had a home. Then this man turned out to be like the rest of the men I'd known, and I soon feared for my life." (This story would go on to express the feelings experienced during the entire incident or story).

Take a few minutes to write your version. It might help to take a look at the list of feeling words on the next page. You may have experienced more feelings than you're aware of.

Feeling Words			
Positive	**Negative**	**Happy**	**Sad**
Glad	Suspicious	Pleased	Lonely
Elated	Bitter	Joyful	Devastated
Excited	Ashamed	Content	Shattered
Proud	Worthless	Cheerful	Depressed
Relieved	Miserable	Grateful	Embarrassed
Inspiring	Nervous	Peaceful	Unaccepted
Daring	Scared	Thankful	Stupid
Loving	Ugly	Protected	Alone
Eager	Embarrassed	Satisfied	Bitter
Confident	Afraid	Hopeful	Furious
Terrific	Fearful	Calm	Lonely
Included	Uncomfortable	Thrilled	Hurt
Valued	Insecure	Giddy	Discouraged
Loved	Anxious	Safe	Despairing
Strong	Worried	Relaxed	Sorrowful
Courageous	Weary	Alive	Forgotten
Prepared	Exhausted	Sparkly	Rejected
Peaceful	Angry	Ecstatic	Injured
Secure	Annoyed	Blissful	Victimized
Positive	Enraged	Content	Tense
Satisfied			
Determined			
Optimistic			
Empathetic			
Concerned			

Write your story:

_____

_____

_____

_____

_____

_____

_____

_____

_____

_____

_____

_____

_____

_____

_____

_____

_____

Section D
Trauma and PTSD from Medical Crises

Jerome watched his son, Jack, race to the end zone in the biggest football game of the year. Here came the pass and—amazingly—Jack caught it right on the goal line! Players from both teams immediately piled on Jack. The ref called the touchdown, and most players started back to the sidelines. But Jack still lay on the field. Oh no! Paramedics were already coming with a stretcher.

That was three weeks ago. Today Jerome paces in Jack's hospital room and waits for him to come out of a deep coma. Nothing's certain. The scene plays over and over in Jerome's head. He can't sleep. He can't stop fidgeting. He snaps at the nurses and doctors with his fists balled in anger and helplessness. The only thing he can do now is pray. "God! You can fix this! You can bring my son back. I'm helpless here. Please bring him back to me."

"Thank God no matter what happens." (1 Thessalonians 5:18)

Do you struggle with this verse? I sure do. But I've learned that the verse doesn't mean we have to be glad about what happened; it does mean we thank God because we know He can get us through and turn all things for good in our lives.

This is such a personal struggle for me. I've cried and pleaded with God in times of great trouble. But so often I've forgotten to thank Him. I didn't even say the words because I was so full of misery.

Now, years later, I can thank God from my heart for how tragedies turned out. I'm still struggling with the "thank-you" on a few of them. I forget that I can say, "God, thank you that you were there with me, thank you that you're with my broken child, thank you for your healing presence." And that's enough.

PTSD and illness or injury

"You have six months to live … at the most."

"Your child can't survive with the heart damage that occurred during delivery."

You get a phone call and learn that your loved one has died in a highway accident.

All these are examples of trauma. The trauma may not occur *to* you, but you are a witness to it, which is also traumatic. That's why Post-Traumatic Stress Disorder can develop in both patients *and* loved ones after injury or serious illness.

I know that some of you are facing serious health situations, like Jerome's son. My heart goes out to you. I pray that you feel God's healing presence, and I pray that you will be healed. Let's talk more about it on my website, listed in the back of this book.

The two stories in this section deal with healing. Both stories contain outcomes that even doctors couldn't explain. Watch for God in these stories. He's there, and you can see Him at work. Watch for the thank-yous, and also the missing thank-yous, which you can add as you take notes.

Miraculous
Peg, in her own words

"You have a zero percent chance of survival."
Just imagine hearing that from your doctor. I did. Fast forward to today: I'm a miracle! A walking, talking miracle. I'm long past that day of zero percent. Here's how it happened.

Several years ago, I was diagnosed with Stage II uterine cancer. The standard of care called for a radical hysterectomy followed by 35 rounds of pelvic radiation. At the end of my treatments, my radiation oncologist said, "Just go back to doing what you were doing before. Eat what you were eating, drink what you were drinking, and think what you were thinking." This turned out to be very bad advice. What I know now—but didn't know then—was that when nothing changes, nothing changes.

In June of 2010, after a chest X-ray revealed something suspicious in my lungs, a CT scan, followed by a needle biopsy, revealed that cancer had metastasized to both lungs. There was a lemon-sized tumor near my heart, a walnut-sized tumor in the back of my right lung, and what the radiologist described as "innumerable tiny tumors" scattered throughout both lungs.

The doctor gave it to me straight, without a flinch, no look of regret or sadness on her face. I had already beaten uterine cancer once. Now it had returned; metastasized to both lungs. She must have been speaking a foreign language because the message did not compute. I couldn't have heard her correctly. Me, dying at age 58, when I had just started living? It couldn't be true.

My husband and I sat paralyzed in our chairs. We could not move from the room while we processed this death sentence. Later, we dubbed the new doctor "Dr. Pit Viper," because she had the bedside manner of a poisonous snake.

After the diagnosis was confirmed, things got even worse. I was "upgraded" from being treated by a gynecological oncologist to treatment by the head of the oncology department at my HMO. During our first and only visit with this doctor, my husband and I were stunned by the detached and dispassionate manner in which he proclaimed my prognosis. "Terminal cancer, zero percent chance of survival, nine-18 months to live, nothing we can do except give you morphine when the pain sets in and connect you with hospice." When I asked him if there was anything I could do to increase my stay time on the planet, he said "Hmm, maybe a little light exercise." Within seconds his hand was on the door, racing to see his next patient.

In the eight weeks of tests leading up to the diagnosis of Stage IV metastatic cancer, I developed what is known as "white coat syndrome." Each office visit or test invariably brought more frightening news—and with it an immediate physical reaction. I would only have to see someone wearing a lab coat or sporting a stethoscope to break out in a cold sweat. I could feel my heart racing, palms and underarms sweating, and my body growing cold in my core—as if I'd swallowed ice cubes. (And, of course, this is precisely when the nurse wanted to take my blood pressure reading!)

Hearing the news that you have terminal cancer is devastating. *How* I received it had a very real—and very negative—impact on both my physical and mental health. I recall visualizing myself in a cave—a safe space. The message sent to my primitive brain by insensitive doctors was this: A bear is entering your cave. There is nothing we can do to protect you from the bear. You are going to die. My physiological response was predictable: anxiety, adrenalin and cortisol rush, depression, hopelessness, disempowerment, fear—all known to impair immune function and increase the body's inflammatory response.

One scientific study has found that over 80% of all new breast cancer patients displayed some kind of PTSD symptoms between the time they were diagnosed and the time they started treatment. I'm not surprised, if their diagnoses were delivered like mine.

A few days later we met with a second-opinion oncologist at the same HMO, upon whom we conferred the moniker "Dr. Benign." I told him I felt traumatized by Dr. Pit Viper's prognosis, and I felt the manner in which she delivered the news was bordering on malpractice. He described himself as a "realistic optimist" and though he concurred with Pit Viper's prognosis, he did allow for the minuscule possibility of spontaneous remission and admitted that "doctors don't know everything."

When asked the same question about what I could do to be proactive, he gave a somewhat more enlightened response: "Live joyfully." Although Dr. Benign could not recommend any effective treatment, by allowing for the remote possibility of outliving my predicted shelf life, I was given a sliver of hope. He was hired. After meetings with both oncologists, I went home and cocooned under the covers of my bed. I also asked my husband to bring me the biggest bottle of Jameson's Irish Whisky he could find.

I was in shock. I stayed in bed for five full days and nights, cold, shaking, sleepless, and semi-inebriated. I couldn't bring myself to tell my adult children, my siblings, or my closest friends about the news. I wanted to isolate and deny. To say the words "terminal cancer" out loud would make them real, and I wasn't ready for that reality.

On the morning of the sixth day, I emerged from my cocoon. I told my husband I wanted to do two things: share the news with my church family and buy some good produce at the Farmer's Market. I had eaten virtually nothing for six days and was starving.

At the Christian church I attend, I recall the part of the service when the pastor asked for prayer requests. A dear friend held my hand to give me the courage to say the words "terminal cancer" for the first time. I left the church knowing that prayers were ascending on my behalf. After church, my husband and I went to the nearby Farmer's Market and purchased two large bags of fresh produce. When I thought we were finished with our shopping, my husband insisted we walk down one last row of vendors.

After a few minutes, we encountered a man selling wheat grass. Although I had no interest in wheat grass, I felt compelled to stop at his booth. He regaled us with the many health benefits of this miracle grass for a minute or two, and then his eyes locked on mine. Looking directly at me, he said "If I had a serious health condition, I would get myself to the Optimum Health Institute in Lemon Grove."

Where did that come from? I hadn't told this stranger anything about being diagnosed with cancer. While I didn't realize it instantly, this was a "God thing."

Throughout my life I've had a belief that all the resources I need come to me precisely when I need them. My husband and I raced home and did an internet search for the Optimum Health Institute (OHI). We learned it was a holistic healing center, located not far from our home in California. They had an open house every Sunday afternoon, so we decided to check it out. During the presentation by one of the facilitators at the health institute, I was struck by how she candidly explained, "We have never healed anyone of anything here. We are not a medical facility and we don't diagnose or treat disease. Instead, we provide the education, tools, and techniques to enable people to heal themselves."

Finally, here was something I could do. Finally, hopelessness was replaced by hope and empowerment. A holistic program acknowledges the inter-connectedness of the mind, body, and spirit. If you have a disease of the body, you cannot be fully healed unless you engage the cooperation and healing of your mind and spirit. My husband and I signed up to attend the following week. By the middle of week one I was already beginning to see improvements in my breathing and coughing so I signed up to complete the entire three-week-long program.

On Wednesday of week one, a woman named Helen from London offered to pray over me. My husband was a witness to this intercessory prayer, along with another couple from Florida. Helen was Syrian by birth and prayed in Aramaic, the language historians believe Jesus and the disciples spoke. We lit a candle and knelt around Helen's bed. I could not understand any of the words Helen spoke, but completely understood the profound feelings of being loved, comforted, and reassured by this intimate prayer circle.

When I understood the mind-body connection, I started giving myself "live" messages instead of "die" messages. I also gave myself permission to expect a miracle, or at least a different outcome from what had been promised by my oncologists.

I was able to eliminate my fear by meeting so many others who had been healed of cancer. I also established a "divine dialogue" through daily meditation. During these times of quiet reflection, I could talk to God. Sometimes, I felt God reassuring me that I'd be okay and not to worry about the cancer. Eliminating fear freed up energy that could be used for healing.

I kept a running list of anything and everything I learned, either from classes or from guests, that might add momentum to my healing. Remember, my oncologists could each think of only one healthy practice to improve my chances for survival. At the end of my stay, my Healthy Living Practices list totaled a whopping 158 items!

I did the residential program week in and week out in a very disciplined and determined way, not allowing myself any cheats, shortcuts, or anything that would compromise my healing. I felt since God had divinely led me to this place, the least I could do was be 100% committed to my new full-time job of healing. The medical results were astonishing: After eight weeks, the largest tumor was gone and the second largest tumor was one-third its original size. After 19 weeks, there was no evidence of cancer.

My miracle occurred during Thanksgiving week of 2010. Since then, I get regular chest X-rays and blood tests to ensure the cancer has not returned. I always experience some level of "scan-xiety" before and after these tests. And whenever I hear that someone I know has had a recurrence, I feel the wash of ice-cube-like cold run through my core, imagining that the next shoe to drop will be mine. I've learned to remind myself in these times that they are not me. I am safe, the bear is nowhere near the mouth of my cave.

And I also try to recall when God spoke to me during a meditation, telling me He put me on earth to walk alongside others on their healing journey. I feel very fortunate that my PTSD symptoms are intermittent and not as debilitating as many other cancer survivors' (about one-third of all cancer survivors experience PTSD).

Because the cancer forced me to reevaluate every aspect of my life, it could be considered a blessing rather than a curse. My husband says it best, "Cancer was the best worst thing that ever happened to us."

I'm now a seven-year cancer thriver and have been employed as the program director at the Optimum Health Institute (http://www.optimumhealth.org/) since 2011.

Advice from Peg
When you get bad news and you think you're going to die, don't give up on life. No one on earth has the ultimate answer in uncertain situations; only God does. So wallow in your sorrow if you need to for a bit (I certainly did). But then choose life. Go after it with all you've got. Use your God-given gifts of intuition, body wisdom, and common sense. Watch for those divine interventions because they will be there.

You may not get the answer you'd hoped for, but you'll get the right answer, and when the answer comes, you will be ready to receive it. To Life!

***

Insights from Peg's Story

How wonderful to hear stories like Peg's. While conventional oncology treatments offer little hope once cancer has metastasized and reached its end stage, many people like Peg have discovered alternatives that have resulted in so-called "spontaneous remissions." Peg bristles at the term, saying "It's insulting to call my healing a 'spontaneous' remission. The word suggests I played no part in my healing, and then one day the cancer simply disappeared. God and I teamed up on this project—He led me to OHI, but I was determined, disciplined, and did the grunt work."

Does miraculous healing occur today?

Yes. Most of us have heard of people who have been healed without medical intervention. It's easier for us to see Jesus stepping in and healing miraculously when there isn't another explanation. Even doctors say they have seen spontaneous healing that they themselves cannot explain.

Yes. In other situations, we see terminal cases of cancer and other diseases "miraculously" healed through medical treatment. Most individuals who have experienced this also acknowledge that there had to be divine intervention to accomplish the healing through prayer, faith, and belief that God would ultimately heal them.

Yes and no. Still another group experiences healing, but may not be set free of suffering. People who have lost a limb and survived may cope with pain and complications for the rest of their lives. Those who have recovered from a car accident but lost a beloved child may be fully healed physically but experience ongoing psychological suffering.

Yes, post-death. We all know of devout believers who do not receive healing. They suffer, and they die—no matter how committed they were to prayer, belief in God's healing power, and miraculous intervention. Physical healing simply didn't take place. Instead, these Christ-followers were healed the second their earthly bodies died; they went to heaven healed and whole.

Dr. Kelly A. Turner[1], author of the book *Radical Remission*, points out there are over 1,000 reports of "spontaneous remissions" that have been documented in the medical literature, but that they weren't being pursued by researchers as to the commonalities among them. She asked the right questions, "Why did each of these people experience a spontaneous remission? Was it spontaneous or was it something they did?"

Dr. Turner found out that their remissions were due to something they *did*. She uncovered nine factors that can lead to a radical remission from terminal cancer—even after conventional medicine has failed. They are: radical change of diet, taking control of treatment, using your intuition, using herbs and supplements, releasing suppressed emotions, increasing positive attitudes, embracing social support, deepening spiritual connection, and having strong reasons for wanting to live.

If you are currently facing the effects of trauma, I hope you'll take a serious look at the nine strategies above. Everyone can work toward releasing suppressed emotions, increasing positive attitudes, embracing social support, deepening spiritual connection, and having strong reasons to live. These are all enriching strategies for making positive changes as you build your new life.

Approach PTSD like cancer?

When Peg began her healing journey, she adopted a holistic protocol that employed all the tools available to her for mind, body, and spirit. The intensive and lengthy program included all nine factors identified above. With the help of her son, she also built a large, electronic support system: the Crazy Cancer Love Train. "Love Trainees" kept up with Peg's process and progress online and sent her a tsunami of love and encouragement through cards and emails. And she was victorious.

What if we approached PTSD the same way? What if we bombarded it with counseling, special therapies like EMDR (Eye Movement Desensitization and Reprocessing) therapy, rounding up a huge support group, daily prayer and meditation, and daily application of strategies for handling flashbacks, depression, anxiety, fear, and the many other intrusive and debilitating symptoms?

Looking back on my own story validates this idea. I developed a plan with my counselor, rounded up strategies to use, gathered an army of prayer warriors, and more. Was I healed? Not completely—yet. But I've moved beyond surviving to thriving, as you read in Sylvie's story, "An Unexpected Deliverance."

I'd like to encourage you to give the "all-out" approach a try. It could take months to see progress, but I believe you will see it. Let's hope together.

Please note: in the story above, the names "Peg" and "Optimum Health Institute" have not been changed. We want readers to know of this tremendous resource that Peg employed in her healing journey.

Next, let's read one story from the viewpoints of four different people. It might be very difficult to read because a child is injured, but I hope you'll give it a try. There is so much we can learn from this story.

A Little Boy Burned
Sadie, in her own words

I'm an old woman now. I can't hear well, see well, or move fast. Only hair dye keeps me brunette instead of gray, or worse—blue. But 41 years ago when I was 27, I was really good looking. Oh, I didn't know it then. I was too worried about how I looked to see the beauty myself ... snappy brown eyes, dark wavy hair, and a curvy figure.

On a Sunday way back then, I was getting our apartment ready for three guests—Maggie and Brian, a young couple my husband and I knew from seminary, and Eli, their two-year-old son. As a shy introvert, I was worried about this visit. *Would I even know how to start a conversation?*

Turns out, I didn't need to worry at all. Eli, Brian and Maggie's lively tow-headed two-year-old marched in the door and took charge of entertainment. His antics and chatter instantly bonded the adults around him, charmed by an adorable toddler who was so cute, very funny, always curious, and such a good kisser with the softest little face. Life had not yet scarred him in any way.

We soon set out to enjoy a sparkling sunny day at an entertainment park. We stayed into the evening, walking, laughing, and eating our way through the gorgeous day. We were all young enough then to stay up late, so we headed back to the apartment for a bite to eat. Little Eli was eager to see our cat again. The cat—not so eager.

Brian, Maggie, and Eli still had to make a long trip back up the coast that night, so we planned on just a quick snack. I set out the pie and ice cream and put a 10-cup coffee pot on the table. I remember pushing the table back toward the wall so I could plug in the coffee pot to keep it hot. It seemed safe there because the space was too tight for anyone to accidentally get near the scalding liquid.

Except for … one tiny boy chasing one running cat.

The cat dashed under the table with Eli hot in pursuit. And then it happened. Either the cat or the boy tripped on the coffee pot cord and toppled the scalding pot off the table. All ten steaming cups gushed right onto the toddler's shoulder and back. No one saw it happen, but everyone heard the scream that followed, and followed, and followed.

Brian raced Eli into the bathroom to immerse him in the tub, drape him with wet towels … anything to stop what had happened, and was still happening. Screaming, burning little boy. Anguished, terrified adults.

In a few minutes, Brian tore out of the bathroom with Eli swaddled in towels and still screaming. Brian tossed his car keys to my husband, and the three of them raced off to the hospital. The silence in the apartment was suddenly deafening.

I truly didn't understand—or didn't want to understand—what had happened. But the boy's mother, Maggie, knew. "We've got to get to the hospital!" she shouted. But which hospital? "Let's just go to the closest one!" she said, already on her way out the door.

We sped to the nearby hospital only to learn the threesome had been sent to another hospital near downtown. A hospital with a burn unit.

Back then, there was no GPS, cell phone, or texting. We were all on a desperate mission to save a little boy, and all operating in the dark. Finally, we found University Hospital. I dropped Maggie off at the Emergency Room, then found a place to park.

By the time I got to the ER, only my husband was there. "Eli is in the burn unit, and they're doing everything they can for him." Actually, I'm guessing at this part because here my memory stalls. I have three clear memories of all the frantic weeks that followed. I remember:

- Making food for several days for people at our apartment and other people at the hospital
- Calling my boss at a new job to beg for a few days off He was skeptical.
- Visiting Eli just once, standing back and watching others play with him. He was dabbing lip balm on everyone's lips—fun for him and good exercise for his left arm, which was braced up high so his skin could stretch as it healed. The sight overwhelmed me with regret and grief that this little boy was now terribly blemished, and I had played a role in it. I stepped behind a room divider to cry. Brian brought Eli over to show me how well he was doing, but I had come undone and turned away. I turned away from a little boy who needed love and laughter. How selfish I was. But I was trapped by the trauma this small boy now faced because of scalding burns from a hot brew that I myself had made

I remember nothing else of the many long weeks this precious young family had to stay in our town, the many long months—and years—that the little boy suffered. Brian and Maggie had been on their way to an assignment as missionaries in Medellin, Colombia. Now delayed, of course. Eli was in the hospital for weeks; I don't think I ever went back to take him a toy or to tease out a smile.

Did we stay in contact with Brian and Maggie while they lived in our city in the midst of a tragedy? I have no idea. When did they finally leave? What were the degrees of Eli's burns over what percent of his body? I couldn't tell you.

I remember seeing Eli twice in the years that went by. Once as a sleeping five-year-old; I couldn't see the burns. Later, as a handsome 10-year-old. I couldn't see the burns under his shirt, but I asked if I could talk with him. I told Eli that it was the coffee I made that had burned him. I told him I was very, very sorry, that it never should have happened. I think he understood

I was asking for forgiveness but not using that word because what had happened at my hand was unforgivable.

Years later, I contacted Maggie and Brian when I knew I wanted to include Eli's story in this book. Maggie reminded me that they also planned to use the story in a book. Then she said, "But it's your story too."

So I wrote it as my story. It was only then—just as I started to write—that I realized what had happened to me in Eli's story. I disappeared from it. It was too much to bear. I put the heartbreak away so I could survive my day-to-day life. I *dissociated*, or set up an invisible, impermeable wall between me and that tragedy. I kept it up for weeks and months that grew into years and years.

I have felt the heaviness in my heart about what happened for decades. Who wouldn't? But just now I see God bringing the details back to life because I can bear to know about them today. PTSD always brings up past trauma. God used my PTSD to bring up Eli's story. By showing me my own broken life, I see that God held me in His arms when I was about to lose myself. Through this process, He is filling in the blanks in circumstances I've experienced. He's making me more like me and, maybe, more like Him.

Advice from Sadie

Whatever age we are, God can heal the hurts from any of our past years. He's healing my childhood and early adult years through experiences like this surprise when I sat down to write. He can heal the younger versions of "you," too. This gives me hope for Eli, who is now a handsome, hard-working man with a beautiful family. I pray that God will heal the many hurts that must have come from the tragedy when he was just two years old.

***

Insights from Sadie's Version of the Story
Dissociation

In dissociation, a person doesn't integrate certain experiences or time periods into their sense of self. This results in the person "forgetting" what happened as a way of distancing from something that is too hard to bear.

Dissociative Amnesia

It's interesting to note that Sadie did not dissociate while she had critical tasks to do. When her last critical task was complete (getting Eli's mother to the hospital), Sadie's overwrought emotions could finally "take Sadie away" from the trauma and give her some much needed space to recover, so her regular life of working and homemaking didn't fall completely apart. She probably appeared rather normal to others during the next several weeks, because she could function in the moment. But the moments weren't being processed mentally or emotionally, and so later she couldn't retrieve memories of the weeks following Eli's trauma. The memories weren't "filed" like normal memories are. When people don't register reality, they have what is called "dissociative amnesia."

Sadie had earlier traumas in her life in which she learned to dissociate for survival. Then, through the rest of her life, dissociation became a natural coping mechanism. While it wasn't a healthy way to cope, Sadie didn't realize she was doing it. Neither did anyone around her, so she mostly appeared to act and respond in a normal fashion.

Are you in a story like this?

Do you recognize yourself in Sadie's story? If you've used dissociation to cope, that's okay. In fact, dissociation is the only way many children who experience trauma can survive. To them, it's a gift that allows them to put the hurt away and carry on with life. The difficulty comes later, when adults who have dissociated suddenly recall a traumatic memory or event from their childhood. Then they must reexperience the event and deal with it as the trauma that it was at the time it happened.

So if you find that you've used the strategy of dissociation, don't be hard on yourself. You did it as the only way through an experience that was otherwise impossible to survive. If this is true for you, I hope you'll take the time to work with a counselor to process the "forgotten" memories. Dissociation could be a valuable clue to your past and offer an opportunity to heal from memories you've filed away.

A Little Boy Burned
Maggie and Brian, in their own words

Maggie: Sadie remembers that night far differently than we do. I remember that night and the days following with remarkable clarity even though it's been more than 40 years since that life-altering event. What I remember most clearly, in addition to our concern about Eli, were the many ways we saw evidence of God's loving care and unfailing faithfulness during those days in the hospital and the months that followed.

Brian: Maggie, Eli, and I were in California visiting my family for Christmas. That was our last U.S. stop before our young family of three was to head out for language study in Costa Rica.

We took a day to drive down the coast to visit friends, Sadie and Tim, and to go to an amusement park. After the park and dinner, we went to our friends' home for dessert. That's when disaster struck. Eli was following Sam the cat around the dining room table. Our beautiful boy tripped over the cord to the coffee pot and 12 cups of boiling coffee poured onto his shoulder, face, neck, and back. Eli began to scream, and I jumped up, grabbed him, and raced into the bathroom where I ran cold water over his back to stop the burning. I then took off his shirt and watched the skin just peel away from his back.

My friend Tim said, "Brian, we need to go to the hospital now!" He and I ran with Eli to the car and raced to the ER at the closest hospital. After evaluating Eli's condition, the medical staff told us that the burns were more than they could handle and that Eli and I would be taken to another hospital by ambulance. My first thought was, "How can it be that a hospital in the United States isn't able to care for his burns?" We were supposed to leave for Costa Rica in a few days, and I would have expected that kind of statement there. But we didn't yet realize how serious the burns were.

So off we went. Eli was crying, "Make it stop, Daddy! Make it stop!" But I couldn't do a thing except say to the Lord, "God, Eli is yours. We gave him to you when he was born, and we renew that commitment right now. If he lives, help us through this horrible situation; if he dies, give us the strength to deal with that. Your word says to give thanks in all things, and so I thank you as an act of trust in you." At that moment there was a deep sense of peace and assurance that came over me that I can't explain. I still didn't know if Eli would live or die, but I knew that we would get through that experience with God's help.

Maggie: As Brian ran out of the house with our precious little boy, and I prepared to follow in another car, our friends came close to comfort me and pray for our family. I remember feeling the presence of God surround me with inexplicable peace as I prayed——or was it the Spirit praying? "Father, thank you that you are with us no matter what lies ahead."

Brian: The ambulance took us to University Hospital, which I later learned was a teaching hospital and had one of the finest burn units in the world. As the doctors began to work on Eli, they asked where we lived. I told them that we were essentially homeless as we were on our way to Costa Rica where we would be studying Spanish for a year.

At that point they looked up and informed me that we would not be going anywhere for several months. With grave expressions, they said that since 16% of Eli's body was severely burned, he would spend at least three weeks in the intensive care unit for burn victims. The doctor explained that burns like Eli's send the skin cells into shock for at least three weeks. Then the cells would begin to respond to treatment and start healing. The treatment and care phase would entail from several weeks to several months of skin grafts, plastic surgery, counseling, etc. Hearing that sent me into shock. But I still had that peace inside.

Maggie: By the time I got to the hospital, little Eli was already sedated, lathered in zinc oxide, and asleep. I spent some time watching him sleep and praying for my precious little baby. After a while we decided it would be best for me to try to sleep at Sadie's house to be ready for the following day. So I went back to Sadie's where sleep eluded me, but God's peace comforted my soul. Brian stayed at the hospital on a gurney close to Eli in case he woke up frightened or disoriented in the night.

Early the next morning I was back at the hospital in time to watch the staff do the daily task of "debriding," cleaning dead skin and unhealthy debris from Eli's burns by washing them and using surgical instruments and brushes. Because Eli was so tiny, they put him in a large sink of warm water and meticulously pulled off the dead skin.

As the debriding happened, Eli silently held onto his daddy's fingers as tears streamed down his cheeks. Afterwards his daddy's big hands would reach out and pick Eli up to comfort him. That gave me a mental picture of our little family resting in God's hands, our place of safety and comfort.

Brian: To be with Eli in the burn-care unit, we had to put on gowns, booties, caps, and masks as well as scrub our hands with a special disinfectant soap. It was a lengthy process, but so necessary. What I experienced when I entered the burn unit took me by surprise. Most of the burn victims were horribly scarred with disfigured faces, hands, arms, and legs. I was repulsed by what I saw and wanted to shut the sights out of my mind. I was struck by the fact that in comparison, Eli's burns seemed insignificant. I felt guilty that Eli's condition wasn't worse.

Because Sadie's parents were arriving for a visit, we needed to find a place to stay while Eli was in the hospital. Tim gave me the name of his landlord and said that perhaps this man would know of someplace where we could stay.

I called the number and told the landlord who I was and what our situation was. He said, "Brian, you don't know me, but I know who you are. We are members of the same church denomination. I'm the president of the board of directors of the denomination's retirement home here. We just finished a new block of apartments, and one of the units is yours free of charge for as long as you need it. Also, you're welcome to eat in the dining room free of charge for as long as you're here."

God knew our need and had "prepared" a home in advance for us only 20 minutes away from the hospital!

Maggie: God's unfailing faithfulness and great love for us was evident in the tender care and kindness each of us received in so many ways during those difficult days. As family, friends, and missionary colleagues around the world heard about Eli, people began to pray. We were comforted and grateful to know they were holding us up before God. Later we would see more evidence of the results of these prayers.

Every day we got up early to drive to the hospital to be there before Eli woke up. We spent the whole day and into the night in the hospital, only leaving after Baby Eli was asleep for the night. Because we assumed we would be there for months, we began to think of the hospital as God's new call on our lives, and we looked for ways to engage in the lives of those around us.

After a few days, Eli was allowed outside the burn unit. There, we met the parents of two little girls who had been horrifically burned in a camper explosion. I was so sad to also hear that the girls' mother had a miscarriage as a result of the trauma of the explosions. It was such a poignant moment when she showed me a picture of her beautiful little girls before the accident.

Brian: Five-year-old Dawn was the older of the two sisters, with burns over 75% of her body. Her face was unrecognizable. She was back in the hospital for ongoing plastic surgery. God placed on our hearts the need to talk with this family and to pray for them.

Because Dawn's burns were so intense and covered so much of her body, it was important that she move and talk. If not, eventually the scarring would inhibit movement and cause the muscles to atrophy. Outside the burn unit, there was more room for Dawn and the others to play, move around, and engage in conversation. But these poor little ones were in such pain, they mostly just sat and watched as Baby Eli toddled around. Eli was especially drawn to Dawn. Physically she looked monstrous with her badly burned face. But Eli often went to Dawn and kissed her in the hope that she wouldn't be so sad. The exercise was good for Eli, too, and we were glad to see that his loving spirit hadn't been harmed a bit.

Maggie: Somehow, in the process of seeing God at work in the hospital, we became content to be there and started to anticipate what God had in store for us there. We heard about a young Latino man who had been in an automobile accident and was in a coma, not responding to treatment. We were told he could hear what was going on around him. His wife came faithfully every day and talked with her unresponsive husband. Brian talked with him, too, every day, telling him that life was worth living, that Jesus loved him and wanted him to get well. To our great joy, within days the man started breathing on his own and responding. Soon he was moved out of ICU!

Brian: One day I was praying with a group of people, asking God to be with them, to guide the doctors, and to heal them. After I prayed, an older woman asked me, "You were praying for me, weren't you?" I was, and I told her so. Though by faith tradition she was Jewish, she asked me, a young Christian missionary, to pray with her again before her cancer surgery. The surgery went well, and we became good friends and stayed in touch for many years after.

Maggie: Just a week after the accident, we had a big surprise. When we got to the hospital, we found that Eli had been moved to the pediatric ward! When we got to Eli's new room, he was sitting on his bed with huge bandages making him look like a miniature Michelin Tire Man. We waited for the doctor to talk with us, and when he arrived, he was almost speechless. "I have absolutely no explanation for why Eli is healing so much faster than normal," he said. "In fact, there's really no need for Eli to be in the hospital any longer except to come in for daily debriding." We were floored! "I've never seen a case like this, and I've never had a patient like Eli," finished the doctor, shaking his head.

Oddly, we had mixed feelings. We were thrilled that Eli was healing far ahead of schedule, but we were also a little sad that our ministry time in the hospital was coming to an end so quickly.

Brian: The next day, the staff told us Eli didn't have to come back for two days, and at the end of the week we were told to come back in a week! Incredibly, three weeks after the burn, the staff informed us that Eli's burns were completely healed with no danger of infection. We were released to go anywhere in the world! The three-to-six months of intensive care, skin grafts, and therapy were reduced to one week of intensive care, and a mere month before we were on the plane for language study in Costa Rica. It was nothing short of amazing.

As Eli was being released from the hospital, I received a summons to meet with the head of the burn unit. I was a little apprehensive because of the doctor's reputation for being gruff. But to my surprise, the doctor said, "Brian, this has been an unusual case. We've never seen a patient and family so positive and helpful to others, and we've never seen any burn victim heal so quickly with so little residual effects from the burn. I just want you to know that I am not charging you for my services. Call it a professional discount."

What?! This was beyond belief. In fact, no matter how many times I tell the story, I am amazed at how God cared for us and transformed a disaster into an example of God's grace and care.

Maggie: People sometimes ask us how it was that we could have faith in the light of Eli's suffering. But in reality, our faith in the loving care of God was our only refuge and source of hope. Before Eli was born, we had seen God's loving care and faithfulness in our lives, both individually and as a couple. So we chose to make what you could call "daily deposits" into a "faith account." Those daily deposits had to do with choosing to trust God, choosing to believe in God's sovereign plan for our lives, choosing to believe that God was with us even when life was throwing some pretty difficult circumstances in our direction. So, when Eli was burned, we had already built up a "faith account" to draw on. Facing such a difficult trauma as Eli's burns would have looked and felt completely different if we had not been living in that faith for many years before we needed to draw on the faith account.

A truth we have discovered is that choosing to trust God's unfailing love and faithfulness in crisis, as well as in joyful times, helps us see all the ways God is continually blessing us. During and after our hospital experience, we were blessed beyond belief. In Costa Rica, we hit new hurdles. It was difficult to be in a new culture, learn a new language, and care for a little boy who had undergone so much trauma and was still in pain. But God turned each hurdle into a source of blessing!

It was not easy to see our precious little baby boy suffer. It was not easy to have all of our plans changed in the twinkling of an eye. It was not easy to walk the long path of healing after Eli was released from the hospital, the months when he had to wear a pressure suit to reduce scarring. It was not easy to see Eli's scarred shoulder (where the burn was the most intense) every time his shirt was off over many years. We continued to ask God questions, and it seemed that his answer was always a reminder: We needed to trust daily in God's sovereignty and to remember those who were still suffering from their burns. In our weakness, our faith grew.

We had never heard of PTSD, so we were never aware of what we were probably experiencing. In Costa Rica we found a community of friends who supported us, prayed for and with us, and walked with us through times of frustration and questioning. Though we saw and experienced "miracles," we still found ourselves wondering why some of our prayers weren't answered in the ways we expected. Even so, we continue to trust recklessly in God, no matter how puzzling a situation might be. Choosing to trust is not always easy, but our experience has been that God is always faithful.

Brian: Looking back, I think that we were probably very self-centered, not thinking about the ways others might have suffered. How did this affect our friends? How did it affect our family? Maggie and I never had any feelings of anger or bitterness toward our friends. It was just one of those things that happens. If anything, I felt I was to blame for not keeping a better eye on Eli as he was playing.

In closing, I want to share about one of the biggest blessings that came out of this entire situation. When Eli was in the hospital, my brother Jack came to visit us and to see Eli. Little did we know, Jack had decided to check out of life. He was going to leave his wife, his two children, and their life together and just give up. But Jack's visit to the hospital that day reminded him of what's really important, and he changed his decision to leave his family and throw his life away. It was a secret he kept for years and years, and such a deep blessing when he finally told us.

You just never know what God's going to do.

Advice from Maggie and Brian

What our family went through was traumatic. It was unexpected, could have resulted in death, and changed our world dramatically. But everyone's story is unique. Even if you have strong faith in God, medical and therapeutic intervention can be absolutely essential.

In the midst of trauma, try not to withdraw from others or reject the kind of help they offer. When you turn to God you're not ignoring, denying, or hiding from the reality of emotional, spiritual, and relational scarring that often happens as a result of traumatic events. Turning to God means turning toward our humanity with confidence that God is present with us through each and every part of trauma and recovery. Try to remember that in the midst of life's beauty and brokenness, God is with you, God loves you, and God is at work transforming all of us into the women and men we were created to be.

***

Insights from Maggie and Brian's Version of the Story
Prepared for trauma?

No one can ever really prepare for trauma. For one thing, you never know if trauma is coming at all, and if it comes, what form it will take. But we can be like lifeguards, emergency room staffers, law enforcement and military personnel, and others who stay in shape and bravely walk into trauma-likely territory. These individuals keep their bodies strong, their minds organized with up-to-date techniques and strategies, and their entire beings ready to respond.

Maggie and Brian's boot camp

Brian and Maggie may not have known it, but they had been preparing for trauma for years before it occurred. They had each accepted a personal invitation from God to become a missionary—to walk into trauma-likely territory. They prepared as they matriculated through seminary, stashing away all sorts of information they would need to know to live successfully in a different culture, speak a different language, and gain people's trust so they could "be Jesus" to those who had never heard of Him. When they were fully prepared, life threw in a twist. The first trauma Maggie and Brian encountered was the heartbreaking, horrifying injury of their very own little son, who sustained scalding burns over 16% of his body.

Put to the test

Suddenly, this young couple was faced with trauma worse than they had ever imagined; trauma that threatened the life of their child. But they had chosen to "live a radical life," a phrase explained by Dan B. Allender[1], Ph.D., in his book *The Healing Path*:

> "By taking the healing path I can become more and more like Jesus by becoming more and more human." He says, "In [Jesus'] life and relationships we discover that being fully human involves living with greater intrigue, imagination, and incarnate care for others."

Becoming more human

Looking back at Maggie and Brian's version of the story, we see that they demonstrated:

- **Intrigue** This couple was intrigued by others and took time to find out more about them. This led to their comforting and praying with dozens of people at the hospital while they also cared for their son.

- **Imagining the unseen** Maggie and Brian looked beyond their situation and asked for the moon: the complete healing of their son, the survival of people who were living on death's door, their eventual travel to Costa Rica where they would begin language school.
- **Incarnate care** This couple took on the sufferings of others, often putting others' needs above their own. They freely gave up their agenda of traveling to Costa Rica to fit into God's detour in a U.S. hospital. There, they didn't ask about the culture or faith background of the people they prayed for; they knew God loved each person unconditionally, so they followed His example. They were there for their seriously injured child during all his waking hours. They rested less so they could be with him more. They encouraged him with laughter, cuddling, play, distraction, and rest.

Battle-tested

Maggie and Brian went to the mission field already battle-tested. They spent decades in drug-infested Medellin, Colombia, then known as the drug capital of the world. In the midst of this trauma-likely territory, they raised three faithful young men who now serve God in ministry in the United States and abroad.

A Little Boy Burned
Eli, in His Own Words

I genuinely don't remember anything … anything … anything about that whole situation.

Well, I do have something, but I don't know if it's a memory or a made-up memory from all the stories I heard. I feel like I have a memory of Sadie's house and the table pushed back against the wall. I see a black cat jump over the cord. Then nothing.

I have no residual pain, nor emotional issues related to my burn. I believe in God's goodness, which enables me to be at peace with that which I cannot control. As far as the burn is concerned, I don't have any negative memories about it. What I do have is the example that my parents set and that I have lived with by their recounting of their experience and their complete surrender to God's will in the midst of their pain.

The burn also let me be part of an amazing situation.

I had an uncle who was pursuing a selfish lifestyle in which he was enveloped in alcoholism. We didn't know it at the time, but he had decided his family was a drag, so was going to leave his wife and two kids. For some reason, he came to see me when I was in the hospital. Years later he told me that in the midst of seeing me suffer, God showed him how precious his own children were. He went home and stayed home; he didn't leave his family! The Lord touched him and transformed him. My uncle has apologized to me because he feels like I was burned for him. You know what? I told him I would go through it all over again if he ever needed me to. And I would.

I remember the prayer my parents prayed over me when I was burned. They acknowledged that I belonged to God, and my life was in his hands. That has given me a different perspective with my daughter. I am privileged to care for her; I get to watch her play. I hope to raise her to be passionate about God and loving, generous, and kind toward others. I know that my daughter is not my own, she is God's; and it is so comforting knowing that she belongs to someone who loves her far more than I ... And I love her with every ounce of my being.

Advice from Eli:

If you are a Christian and encounter trauma, remember that the Lord's not surprised by any of this. The Lord knows and has known that this is coming. He's not surprised. Not that it doesn't hurt. But there's a light at the end of the tunnel because God has good things planned for you.

If you aren't a Christian and encounter trauma, at some point you'll realize that you have no capacity to control your circumstances. The only control you have is over how you respond. As hard as it is, you can respond with a positive approach and a positive outlook. You may be shattered, but you are not unique in your suffering. You a part of a suffering reality that comes from being a human living on earth.

The one thing none of us gets to do ... is to choose not to suffer or to go through difficulties in life.

***

Insights from Eli's Version of the Story
Building resilience

Eli's parents did a good job of raising a resilient child. They approached the traumatic situation matter-of-factly, trusting their faith in God to get them through. The Model Systems Knowledge Translation Center[2] (www.msktcorg) encourages parents of children with severe burns to build resiliency in these ways:

  • Believe in your child's strength ("This is very hard, but I know you will get through it")

- Get your child back into a typical routine as soon as possible; expect your child to follow the family rules about behavior, manners, etc.
- At first, spend extra time with your child having fun and relaxing; but get back into a normal routine as soon as possible
- Be a good role model; eat well, exercise, get enough rest
- Try to express intense emotions away from the child
- Encourage your child's independence and inner strength

You can build resilience too

As adults who have been traumatized, building resilience is a healthy strategy to use in recovery and to help prepare yourself should another negative experience occur in your life. An adult list might look like this:

- Believe in your strength and in God's strength and presence
- Follow a healthy, typical routine that gives your body enough rest
- Incorporate self-care into your life; having fun, relaxing, doing something nice just for you
- Eat well, exercise, get enough rest
- Find a safe place to express your emotions, for example to a trusted friend, a counselor, through writing
- As your inner strength builds, decide on other resilient qualities you'd like to have and work toward them

Your Story
How It Connects to the Rest of Your Life

The writing exercise in the previous section might have been a difficult one for you because it dealt with feelings—feelings that you had to identify, name and actually experience again. So this exercise will give your right brain (the "feeling" side) a break and put your left brain to work. It will ask you to think objectively and logically.

First step

Answer some or all the following questions: (examples of answers are below)

- What are some incidents that happened *before* your trauma story took place, and that have a connection to your story?
- What are some incidents that happened *during* your story, and that have a connection to your story?
- What are some incidents that happened *after* your story took place, and that have a connection to your story?

Example

Brian might have answered the questions above like this:

- **What are some incidents that happened before your story took place, and that have a connection to your story?** "Maggie and I had already dedicated our son to God; we knew Eli was His; we had learned to have faith in God's care for us, no matter the outcome."
- **What are some incidents that happened during your story, and that have a connection to your story?** "The provision of a place to stay and food to eat; Eli's

miraculous recovery; the no-charge medical services; many people who prayed for us; the visit by my brother."

- **What are some incidents that happened after your story took place, and that have a connection to your story?** "The multi-year challenge of Eli's healing; our orientation to a new language and culture; the revealing of the decision made by my brother when he saw Eli in the hospital."

Please keep in mind that Brian had years to process these answers, so do not be discouraged if you have difficulty answering. This is simply a step toward healing. Take the step.

You might find it helpful to draw a chart similar to the one that follows. In the boxes, list incidents before, during, and after the event that had an effect on the people involved or on the outcome.

Second step
Add other events to your story that help tell the "whole" story.

Example

For example, Brian might have written:

"We had no idea how our 'faith bank' or preparation for the mission field would provide us with the strength and know-how to get through Eli's tragic injury. While Eli was healing, God provided us with a place to stay, food to eat, and a huge support system of people who were praying for us. We continued to see miraculous outcomes years after Eli was burned, including my brother's decision to stay with his family and be a good father and husband."

Take a few minutes to write *your* version. It can be very short if you're eager to get on with the rest of the book. You can always come back and expand your ideas.

_____

_____

_____

_____

_____

_____

_____

_____

_____

Trauma and PTSD from Abortion-Related Issues

Sixteen and pregnant. So long ago ... 36 years, in fact. But the minute Pat saw the topic of abortion on the TV news, she was instantly back in that cold, tiled room.

The feelings—physical, mental, emotional, and heartfelt—washed over Pat just as they had when she was 16. And the questions, the many unanswered questions. What had the baby looked like? Was it a girl or a boy? What would her life have been like if she had kept the baby, or given it up for adoption?

Pat's present life was fine in every way—job, church, husband, mother, friend—except one. A nagging emptiness festered in her heart and every so often brought her sobbing to her knees. No one but Pat knew about any of this. She felt alone and bereft.

Abortion, a component of the two stories in this section, is an extremely sensitive issue. If this topic triggers past or current trauma for you, I'm so sorry. If it's too difficult to read, I understand. You may be able to come back to it later.

No judgments are made in these stories, although both storytellers connect their trauma, in part, to abortion. Both stories also have healing outcomes, so keep hope in mind as you read.

Abortion is a medical procedure. On rare occasions it is carried out to save the life of the mother. Yet several factors qualify abortion as an act that can result in trauma.

- Deciding whether or not to have an abortion can be traumatic in itself. Abortion is a major, life-altering decision, and no one knows how the mother will feel after the procedure.
- Going through the process of abortion can be frightening or emotionally upsetting.
- Recovering from an abortion requires physical, mental, emotional, and often spiritual healing.

Abortion is a subject that requires love and compassion when addressed in discussion or writing. Jesus loves each individual who is touched by this topic, especially the children and mothers involved. He wants healing to take place in those hurt by abortion just as much as He holds out healing to others suffering from PTSD for other reasons.

My prayer for you is that you will feel Jesus' healing presence as you read this section.

I Need You to See Me
Melanie, in her own words

I stood desperately silent in the grocery store line in Boulder, Colorado. I needed to call for help to my husband, standing near the door, but I couldn't speak. I couldn't get a word out.

Our adult step-son, who'd asked us for money yet again, had filled two grocery carts to overflowing and wheeled up a third cart, stacked full of meat and seafood. We'd agreed to help him and his family with groceries, but didn't anticipate anything like this scandalous load of food. I needed reinforcements!

But whenever I caught my husband's eye, he just smiled back, patiently waiting. The clerk had rung up one and a half carts, and the total was already up to $300—more than I had brought in cash. I burned my eyes into my husband so he would notice the third cart, but he just watched us passively. My mind screamed for him to rescue me; my eyes begged him to come stop the madness. But he just stooped to pick up one of our grandchildren, never reacting to my terrified, silent plea for help.

Suddenly I became paralyzed with fear. Time stopped.

I was no longer in the grocery store. I'd become a little girl, sitting on the lap of a man I didn't know. The man was touching me inappropriately, and my father sat across from us apparently enjoying watching his friend molest his six-year-old daughter. I pleaded with my eyes for my father to help me, but he just sat and watched.

Slowly I returned to reality. The grocery total was $735.00. I numbly paid with a credit card and stumbled out the door. "Wait!" my husband called. "We're supposed to go to lunch with them."

"No. We're leaving," I said flatly. I was so incredibly angry at my husband that I knew if I said another word, I'd start screaming. We drove the three hours home in silence.

At the house, I started writing furiously in my journal. Two years of Life Skills classes had taught me I'd been "triggered" and needed to figure out where the rage was coming from. Otherwise, I would just unload the rage onto my husband—as I had done so many times before. Flashbacks took me right back to my painful past, which began in Oceanside, California. And here I was again.

I was 50 years old when I stood in that grocery store where the memory of molestation had surfaced. *Why then?* I wondered. I thought back to a therapy group I had been in recently. One of the women shared how she and her sister had pushed a dresser against the door to keep their father out at night. He barreled into the room anyway, determined to get what he wanted from his young daughters.

The woman's story had a significant effect on me. That night, it triggered a recurring nightmare I'd had throughout my adult years. In the dream, I was a child standing on the intricately designed green tiles of our bathroom floor. My father was standing in front of me, and water was dripping off my wet hair. That's where the dream usually ended. But the next day in therapy group, the whole memory opened up to all the details of what happened that night—the terrorizing of a child. Standing in the store was just another example of a memory coming back to me.

In addition to being molested, I had not had an easy childhood in other ways. When I was 10, my mom packed up our entire house while my dad was at work, and we moved in with my soon-to-be stepfather, who was in the military. After my mom married him, we moved from Oceanside to Seattle. You would think that getting away from my abusive father would give me a new start, and things would get better for me. But no.

In my teens I began sneaking out of my house at night to walk to a nearby fort. Neighborhood boys met there to drink beer, smoke pot, and play spades. I eagerly joined right in. Words cannot begin to describe the euphoria I felt the first time I got high. The highs gave me happy feelings I'd never had before. I was hooked.

When I was 16 we left Seattle to go back to Oceanside. I continued to chase that high and began using drugs and alcohol regularly just to shut off the voices in my head. More and more, I gravitated to boys. I got pregnant for the first time when I was 16. I'll never forget how humiliated I was when the boy I was dating threw $75 at me and accused me of wanting to use the money for drugs instead of an abortion. There was no one I could talk to. And after the abortion, my life spiraled further out of control.

As a young adult I went into self-destruct mode for the next 10 years, using drugs and sleeping with numerous men. I freely gave away sex to get love back in return. But that, of course, never happened. I ended up in an extremely abusive relationship with a controlling man who hit me regularly. I lost my identity and my self-respect.

I moved to the high desert to get away from my abuser and became involved with some pretty scary people who were manufacturing large quantities of methamphetamines. It was there that I would stay awake for days on end. During those highs, I called up my friends and family and told them that the world was coming to an end, and if they wanted to live, they needed to drive up to the high desert and get on a space ship. Needless to say, I was on the brink of insanity.

During my late twenties, my old boyfriend brought me back to Oceanside, where our relationship picked up right where it left off. Then, abruptly, he went back to "her." When I got pregnant at the age of 27, I was sleeping with three different men at the same time, and I didn't know who the baby's father was. But I didn't want to have another abortion, and so I just ignored the pregnancy for weeks.

When I finally decided to go through with the abortion, I was well into my fourteenth week. The abortionist brought me in to his office and showed me pictures of his family, saying, "You don't want to bring a child into this world when you aren't ready. You can always have more children."

I believed him and went forward with the abortion.

Somehow, I made it into my fifties. I'd been clean and sober from drugs and alcohol for 22 years. I had become an over-achiever who owned her own home, drove a Mercedes, and worked in management at a prestigious law firm. But a river of rage flowed beneath the surface of my perfect life. At home, I was a completely different person. I flew off the handle at the drop of a hat, going from zero to ballistic in a flash. The angry little girl had become an angry big girl, and my husband bore the brunt of the outbursts, accusations, and blame.

The little girl who had been abused stayed on the inside. She was always afraid, never felt like she measured up, and had built sky-high walls up around her so no one could ever see what she was really hiding. My dad had taught me never to reveal family secrets, and so my childhood remained intact and separate from me, or so I thought. I had never spoken of it, not to anyone, ever.

That desperate and expensive morning in Boulder, I finally realized I needed help. Not only was I trying to hide my past and act like a well-balanced person, but I also had a disabled son to care for. Elisha was 19 years old at the time. I'd had three miscarriages during my marriage, and finally my beautiful baby boy, Elisha, made it into the world. But he was damaged and premature. My two earlier abortions were the cause. My doctor said the second abortionist had scraped too deeply into the uterine wall, causing the lining to thin out. Elisha was born three months early and had severe disabilities—all my fault. God was punishing me, so I shook my fist at Him and said, "If that's the kind of God you are, I'm not interested!"

Looking back at Elisha's early days, you can imagine the planning and jostling it took to raise a disabled child. And not just to raise him, but to lavish unconditional love in every way, providing him with the best we could find in treatments, toys, experiences, and life in general.

Back when Elisha was only a year old, God made it clear that I wasn't doing enough—or, maybe I wasn't doing the right things. I was ridden with guilt and shame. One day at church I came face-to-face with a woman I had avoided like the plague. She was head of an abortion alternative clinic, and I expected that she would only load on more guilt.

But the woman was surprisingly understanding. She invited me to a weekend for women who suffer from Post Abortion Syndrome (PAS). I walked away with some incredible tools that helped me reconcile with God. I finally understood that we all have consequences for our actions. In other words, we can choose our sin but we can't choose the consequences. A year later, I began co-leading workshops with the woman I once avoided.

Time went by, and Elisha was soon 19 years old. The dentist discovered that Elisha had four impacted wisdom teeth and three impacted molars, one of which was wrapped tightly around by a major nerve. To remedy this, our doctor referred us to a specialist who, we assumed, would do the procedure in the hospital. But no, the specialist said it could be done out-patient. On the day of surgery he told us that he would not only be doing the surgery, but also administering the anesthetic. Oh how I wish I had listened to the little voice of warning.

"He's all ready to go," announced the specialist two hours later. We took Elisha home, but he was unrecognizable! He was bleeding profusely; we couldn't get it to stop. He had two black eyes, a huge black-and-blue bruise that ran from his cheek all the way down his neck, and giant hematomas on his lips.

We were overwhelmed by the care Elisha needed. We called the doctor, only to learn he had left the country for a vacation. We couldn't reach the back-up doctor. Four days later, we took Elisha to the ER. His temperature was 102.6 and he was in respiratory distress. The doctors determined that he had breathed blood into his lungs and had double aspiration pneumonia. "He may not make it," the doctor said gravely. And he was right. Elisha was soon on his way to his heavenly home.

I came undone after Elisha's death. I had visions of his swollen face taunting me, blaming me. The entire first year was a blur. I received medication for situational depression. Finally I was able to go back to work part-time.

But nothing mattered to me anymore. I had lost my purpose. So I opened God's Word and cried out, "I need you! Please heal my broken heart."

Before long, God began speaking life into me, filling the empty spaces of my soul. The gaping hole in my gut that the wind had been whipping through was being filled up with goodness and His faithfulness. For the first time in my life, I let my guard down and leaned into my Savior.

I started writing beautiful devotions that were meant just for me. But God opened doors to share them with others: the moms in the Bible study at work, other moms who had lost children, and—most of all—my husband. As God healed me, he healed our marriage. He took the broken pieces of my life and put them back together. At this writing, I am getting ready to send the 365 days of devotionals off to be published. In closing, I will share one of my favorite devotionals here.

Devotional by Melanie (excerpt)

"Through Jesus, therefore, let us continually offer to God a
sacrifice of praise—the fruit of lips that openly profess His
name."

(Hebrews 13:15, NIV)

Recently, I was sitting with my little two-year-old
granddaughter, the daughter of one of two adopted sons. She
gingerly held in her little hands the cross with angel wings that
hung around my neck and holds some of the ashes of my child.
She looked up at me and said, "I like this, Grandma, what is it?" I
began to tell her what it was and she asked, "Who is Elisha?"

I took out my phone and showed her the video that my other
adopted son had made for me—a collage of pictures of Elisha set
to a beautiful song, "Dancing in the Sky," that was played at his
celebration of life.

When the video finished playing, she looked at me and said,
"Oh that's Elisha, let's watch it again!" Oh how my heart soared
with gratitude as I sat with this beautiful child on my lap watching
the video over and over again with tears rolling down my face,
singing the song and looking at the pictures of my son. I was with
someone who was interested in seeing him, someone who said
his name, someone who was content with just listening to the
music that was on my phone, and in my heart. And when it was
over, she would look at me and say, "Again, Grandma, again."

***

Insights from Melanie's Story

Not everyone who has an abortion experiences severe trauma. If
Melanie's story was difficult for you to read, and you have had an
abortion-related experience, it could be due to some of the
factors below.

Some women are more likely than others to experience trauma with abortions. You may see your circumstances on the list below. That's okay. It doesn't mean anything is wrong with you, we're simply taking a look at why some things in life are more difficult for some people than others.

Women are more likely to have trauma associated with abortion if they:

- Are terminating a wanted pregnancy
- Feel pressure from others
- Receive opposition from family and friends
- Lack social support
- Have low self-esteem, a pessimistic outlook, little control over life
- Have mental health problems and feelings of stigma
- Have a high need for privacy
- Have been exposed to antiabortion picketing
- Use avoidance and denial
- Feel ambivalent about abortion
- Feel unable to cope with the abortion
- Have had one or more prior abortions
- Have late-term abortions
- Are teenagers
- Are having non-elective (therapeutic or coerced) abortions

If you see yourself in the list above and you're struggling with emotional or physical effects of your, or a friend's, abortion, please don't panic or feel badly about yourself. In fact, good for you for taking an honest look. Now may be a good time to get some professional help to work through your feelings.

Tools for reconciling what has happened

Melanie mentioned that Life Skills provided tools that helped her reconcile her relationship with God. If this is something you believe you need in your life, I've included some simple—but very effective strategies below. These strategies are good for anyone who has experienced trauma or PTSD, not just abortion-related trauma. I hope you'll try them.

- **Think back:** When you experience depression or pain that comes "out of the blue," think back to dates that were significant around the time of the trauma. For Melanie, those dates might include when she had abortions, the due date of the aborted child, and the child's birthdays if the baby had lived. Knowing these dates might help you pinpoint the source of your sadness.
- **Be prepared for triggers:** The sound of a drill or experiencing a medical procedure can trigger flashbacks to the abortion experience. Prepare yourself for these if you can. If the triggers surprise you, thank God that your baby is safely in heaven, being loved by the God of the universe.
- **Give back:** Could you donate time at a pregnancy center? Or donate funds to an organization that offers pregnant women other options besides abortion? You will feel close to your lost child when you help give other children a chance at life.
- **Read comforting Scripture:** The Bible is full of stories about people who were redeemed by God after acting outside His will or expectations. Read about David in the Psalms, get comfort from many verses in Isaiah, and find inspiring stories in the New Testament. Remember that God was with you when the event occurred. He loved you then, and He loves you now.
- **Write out your story:** You can refer to the writing exercises in this book if you're not sure where to start.

Writing will help you work through the emotions, put the past to rest, and remember that God is always with you.

- **Call out to God:** In moments of deep sorrow or grief, call out to God. He wants to hear you at those times and provide comfort to you. Take some quiet time alone to listen to what God may have to say.
- **Cultivate supportive friendships:** Build a network of friends who understand your pain and are willing to listen to your story over and over again. Contact these friends when you feel overwhelmed. Pray with them.
- **Take time to grieve:** You've experienced a loss, and healing requires grieving. Consider these stages of grief and think about where you may be in the process: denial, anger, bargaining, depression, guilt and shame, acceptance.

Trauma and dissociation

This book refers to trauma and dissociation in other places. Here, we are taking a closer look at childhood sexual abuse, the atrocity that was done to Melanie by her father and his friends, in the second case with her father's eager approval. What a truly heinous trauma and betrayal.

Sexual abuse involves every sense (touch, taste, smell, sound, and sight). It occurs when the victims are frightened almost out of their minds, and details are branded into deep memory. But will they remember? Perpetrators gamble that children will not remember, or at least will not tell—either because they don't yet have the language skills, or because they've been frightened with the threat of a grisly punishment.

These children grow into adults and often, at some point, memories that have been dissociated (buried deep in the subconscious) are triggered by life in the real world. Suddenly—in the midst of a grocery store, singing an "oldie," not being able to catch your husband's eye—the past finally demands the attention it should have had for decades. And it often shatters these adults who repressed their painful childhood and now must save their own lives.

Many of the women who have been shattered walk dazed in your church, grocery store, or neighborhood. They're in therapy groups, on Facebook, and in blogs. They might live right next door. Sometimes, Jesus is the only one who sees the shattered pieces in these people.

Please don't be afraid to ask how someone is doing, or if they would like to go for coffee. Talking about what happened and shedding tears over it are prerequisites for most victims' healing.

Remember that these adults were once children who make the statistics below come to life:

- Approximately 4 million child maltreatment referral reports are received by authorities each year.
- These children suffer from one or more of these issues: neglect, physical maltreatment, and psychological, emotional, and sexual abuse.
- Almost five children die every day from abuse.

Child abuse crosses all socioeconomic and educational levels, religions, ethnic, and cultural groups. [1]

Life Skills

Melanie mentions "Life Skills[2]" referring to a 501(c)(3) non-profit educational organization. According to the mission statement, "Life Skills is dedicated to stopping abuse and to teaching the skills that help students uncover root causes of behavior patterns in their lives. At Life Skills, we teach biblically based principles that focus on building character and maturity. Our goal is to help each individual develop 'basic character traits' that will increase their capacity to function in all their relationships and to offer hope of reconciliation whenever possible."

Post-Abortion Stress Syndrome (PASS)

Whatever your opinion on abortion, it is widely recognized that the experience can have significant physical and psychological repercussions. Abortion is seen as a solution to a complex problem, and thus can result in complex outcomes.

Post Abortion Stress Syndrome (PASS) is the name that has been given to the psychological aftereffects of abortion, based on Post-Traumatic Stress Disorder (PTSD). Neither the American Psychiatric Association nor the American Psychological Association has accepted the term "Post Abortion Stress Syndrome." But most experts agree that abortion is never an easy decision, and that a woman gets through it best when she has support and counseling. I hope you'll take advantage of counseling if you or a close friend have had an abortion.

Symptoms of PASS may include any of the following:

- **Guilt:** Experiencing guilt does not imply that you made a mistake. However, feelings around having an abortion may be complex, and may include guilt.
- **Anxiety:** General anxiety is a common symptom of PTSD—in the case of PASS, there might be a particular anxiety over fertility issues and the ability to get pregnant again.
- **Numbness, depression:** Again, common symptoms of PTSD.
- **Flashbacks:** Abortion is surgery, and it often takes place while the patient is conscious. This can be a distressing experience.
- **Suicidal thoughts:** In extreme cases, the PTSD that results from a controversial abortion could lead to suicidal thoughts or tendencies and would require immediate treatment. It's important to note that this is not a common or expected symptom of PASS, but as

with any form of PTSD, it is possible.

Writing

Melanie found that writing is a way to process her inner feelings. Writing can be very helpful to people who have unclear memories of events, who have been through trauma, and who have PTSD. If you get into a safe place, away from interruptions or other people, try writing freely—whatever comes into your mind. You can also write about flashbacks, triggers, nightmares, intrusive thoughts, anger, joy, growth, and healing. Make sure your "internal editor" is turned off. This kind of writing requires only free thinking—no correct grammar or punctuation is needed.

As your hand writes, the thoughts and ideas may flow from your mind, your heart, your spirit, and your deep memories. Just get the words down. Later, you can read over what you wrote. You might be surprised at what you find. Perhaps there will be a thought or idea you'll want to write more about.

This kind of writing can be calming and empowering. These are your feelings, your experiences. They may be sad or joyful, horrifying, or reassuring. Write anyway.

How will you use these words, and what can they do for you? Maya Angelou[3], acclaimed author and poet, wrote, "There is no greater agony than bearing an untold story inside you." Write your story and see if this is true for you. For help getting started, you can use the writing exercises in this book or visit my website or Facebook pages (URLs at the back of the book).

All the Little Babies
Sharon, in her own words

A soft weight rested in my hand. I glanced down. Tiny fingers, a few toes, part of a miniature torso. It's a baby, I realized. But it's too little to be a baby. And where are its... I jerked awake at the scream, and the scream was me. "NO, NO, NO! It's too late. Oh no."

The nightmare reflected my reality when I was just 16. That year, *Roe v. Wade*, the landmark Supreme Court decision to legalize abortion on demand, went into effect. I was a high-schooler, working my first job in a large metropolitan hospital.

I worked in a lab that became increasingly involved with the examination of aborted babies. We had to determine if the fetal tissue (arms, legs, heart, etc.) was present, and if the placental tissue was normal. We had to rule out a condition of the placenta that could result in complications and health risks for the mother, so she could receive proper treatment if needed.

Obviously, an abortion affects the woman having the procedure in many ways. But in addition, an abortion affects every person who comes into contact with this woman, from the staff members who interview and "prep" her to the workers who sanitize the instruments, to the doctors and nurses who perform the procedure, to the workers who clean up the room after an abortion. It takes an entire crew of adults to end one small life and to document that the "child" never existed.

Every workday as a tender teenager, I held the remains of babies in my hands. The babies ranged in age from five weeks to over eight months. I'd been trained to recognize placental tissue; the body parts were easy to identify. I weighed and measured the tiny bodies of the older babies and also determined their sex.

At age 16, I knew intuitively that something was wrong with this. But to keep my job and avoid losing my mind, I soon came to view these little bodies in my lab as "specimens." How else was I to cope?

I pushed my feelings of disgust, horror, and grief deep inside for many years. I grew older. I kept working in the lab. I married. And then—I desperately wanted a baby of my own.

My husband and I tried for a pregnancy for 18 months. Then we went through many tests. Finally, the doctors told us that we would never be able to have our own child. That shock brought long-buried feelings to the surface. The tiny dead babies seemed to come to life in my mind. I couldn't stop seeing them— hundreds and hundreds of them.

Depression took hold, and I developed thoughts of suicide. I went to work every day and held tiny pieces of cast-off babies. I came home at night grieving for the living baby I longed to have.

My husband couldn't understand why my work was so upsetting and why I couldn't shake the tears, nightmares, and desperation. He refused to let me quit my job. So in December, 1979, I admitted myself to a mental health unit of a local hospital. I was really afraid that I would hurt myself if something didn't change.

In the psych ward of the hospital, I was shunned. Politically, the staff couldn't agree with me that abortion caused anyone harm since it was legally performed in their hospital. So none of the other patients could know why I was there or, in the words of the staff, "Why I thought I was there." They didn't allow me to share what had happened or my feelings about it because it would "upset the other patients."

During my three-month stay the hospital staff convinced me that my depression was really caused by my "rigid religious beliefs, a bad marriage, and a controlling family." So I divorced my husband, walked away from God, walked away from my family, and walked into the world, where I stayed for almost two years. I was still very depressed and depended on antidepressants and Valium to cope. I felt lost, alone, and crazy.

But I wasn't alone. God never left me. So when I reached the next low point, I rededicated my life to Christ. With His help, and the help of a wonderful, compassionate church, I started to put a new life together. I thought I could just put my experiences with abortion behind me. So I did—or at least I tried to. But as hard as I tried to forget the past, the past continued to haunt me. I had flashbacks, horrifying nightmares, and intrusive pictures and thoughts that swirled in endless loops in my head.

Looking back, I can see that I had the symptoms of PTSD. However, the secular mental health community refuses to acknowledge that abortion is a "stressor" event for women who experience the procedure, much less someone working in a lab, so I was never diagnosed.

In 1983, my church offered a nine-month Bible school. I became a student and suddenly, as part of the school's requirements, I had to choose a ministry to participate in weekly. I didn't have a clue what to do, so I offered to assist one of the pastors.

After a few months the pastor told me that a Pregnancy Resource Center had requested a liaison from our church. Because of my background, he immediately thought of me. "You've got to be kidding!" I said. "You want me to go to a place that would hold constant reminders of my past? No way."

The pastor was surprised at my response, but asked me to pray about it. While I agreed to pray, I silently told myself—and God—that this was *not* what He wanted me to do!

I continued to resist even the possibility of being involved in this ministry until the Lord spoke loudly and clearly through His Word. I had been reading the book of Isaiah as part of my studies. When I came to chapter 54:1, I saw the verse God had written for me:

> Sing, barren woman, who has never had a baby.
> Fill the air with song, you who've never
> experienced childbirth!

You're ending up with far more children
   than all those childbearing women. GOD says
so!

When I finished reading that chapter, I knew what God had
called me to do.

I was immediately inspired to set up a new ministry called
"Silent Voices." I could be an advocate for saving children
instead of a lab rat who examined babies after it was too late for
them to live! Within six months, I was in full-time ministry as
director of Silent Voices, having written a curriculum for
pregnant women who feel they have no options besides abortion.

No longer did I shove the pain deep down inside me. Instead,
I used the pain to fuel my overwhelming desire to save unborn
babies' lives and to set women free from the guilt and shame that
can follow an abortion. I was still in a lot of emotional pain
myself, but over time God provided healing through a Christian
counselor, hours of reading and meditating on the Bible, and my
own reading and research into Post Abortion Trauma.

That research also helped me better understand and
empathize with women who had chosen to have an abortion. All
the anger I had felt for them melted away as I realized the truth
that "sin is sin." My sin is no different from anyone else's. We all
need the love and forgiveness of the Savior, no matter what
we've done. As I healed, I developed a weekend retreat that has
helped hundreds of women break free from shame, fear, guilt,
and regret. (Look for this retreat on my website,
www.silentvoices.org.)

Today I am still deeply affected by images associated with
abortion. The bloody snapshots in my mind will never go away.
Deep emotions of despair, horror, and trauma can still be
triggered by a sight, smell, word—almost anything. But these
emotions don't control my life anymore! When the nightmares
return I know, now, where they're coming from. I can wake up
confident that I don't have to give in to the feelings that come

with them.

I have been blessed to be in pro-life service since 1984, and I have seen God fulfill all the promises He made to me in Isaiah 54! I have never remarried or had children of my own, but thousands of children around the world are alive now because Silent Voices gave their mothers help, hope, and strength to say no to abortion. And countless women have been set free from the guilt and grief of an abortion because of the healing that God has done in my life and the program He helped me write 30 years ago.

Author's note: This story uses Sharon's real name because some readers may want to consult with her or visit her website, www.silentvoices.org .

Advice from Sharon

I wish I could speak with you, dear reader, in person. You could be someone who's thinking about having an abortion or someone who's had an abortion. You might have a lover, wife, friend, or family member who's had an abortion. Maybe you're a lab worker or a medical doctor who performs abortions. You could be pro-life or pro-choice. Whoever you are, I can say one thing that is true for you, and for me, too. God loves you, and God loves the babies who have been lost. Circumstances don't matter. God loves you. If you want to explore this further, please contact me at my website, Silent Voices (www.silentvoices.org). I would love to speak with you in person and help bring healing into your life.

***

Insights from Sharon's Story
Background on *Roe v Wade*
- **1971 -** The case was filed by Norma McCorvey, known as Jane ROE, against Henry WADE, the district attorney of Dallas County. Wade had enforced a Texas law that

prohibited abortion unless necessary to save a woman's life.

• **January 22, 1973** - The US Supreme Court, in a 7-2 decision, affirmed that it is legal for a woman to have an abortion, citing the Fourteenth amendment to the Constitution. The ruling allows for abortion throughout pregnancy, with conditions that allow states to regulate abortion during the second and third trimesters.

Disposing of or honoring the aborted ones?

Many, if not most, medical personnel who examine aborted fetal tissue find ways to cope with participating in something that they may believe is very wrong. Some distance themselves mentally and emotionally. Others find ways to show respect to the mutilated little bodies, maybe by wrapping them in cloth inside a plastic bag and freezing them (a kind of "burial") instead of disposing of them in waste bins or by incineration. Very recently, the issue of disposing of fetal tissue has risen to state levels. Some states now require burial or cremation of aborted fetuses.

Coping with trauma and controversy

When confronted with horror, atrocities, torture, and other traumas beyond belief, some people turn away. They refuse to see it. Others hide it. They push it out of their minds and refuse to see the images. Still others, like Sharon, push the feelings down deep inside. People who use these strategies often don't begin healing until they bring the trauma out into the light and begin dealing with the horror. Prominent author and expert in trauma and abuse, Dan B. Allender[1] says:

> Suffering sets into motion our will to find
> meaning; it compels us to honestly assess the facts
> of our lives and begin to order truth into a
> framework that has personal meaning to us.

The abortion issue carries a special tension when some see it as an atrocity, and others see it as a necessity. A similar example is the widespread disagreement today about the end of human life: should people be allowed to determine the time, place, and method of dying? Exactly what constitutes death—no brain function? No breathing? No pulse?

The issue of abortion is also rampant with opposing viewpoints. Should a teen carry a baby to full term if she's not prepared to be a parent? Should "defective" babies be aborted? What do we do in situations involving rape?

In the psychiatric facility, Sharon was caught in the crossfire of opposing opinions and, as a result, received no help in recovery. No matter what our current views are about any controversial subject, we must remember the hearts of the people involved. You are not a "statistic" or an "issue." You deserve to be helped through a traumatic experience, supported by the medical community, therapists, and others.

A traumatic training ground?

Author and trauma expert Diane Langberg[2] says:

> Participation in God's work requires that we know how to do what He has called us to do well.... It matters.

Could it be that Sharon's work in the lab—although gruesome and grossly against God's purpose for babies was a sort of training ground, a prep school, for her later development of the Silent Voices organization? Who else could have the intimate knowledge of all aspects of abortion that Sharon developed? God helped her transform her pain into purpose. And look what came of it all.

One thing is certain: Sharon didn't run away from her pain. As she said, "I used the pain to fuel my overwhelming desire to save unborn babies and to set mothers free from guilt and shame." Can you do this in your circumstances? Fueled by pain, and with God's help, you might accomplish brave and compassionate goals beyond that which you ever imagined.

God promises that He can eventually turn our pain into purpose—into some type of action or attitude that can help others who now suffer what we suffered in the past. In 2 Corinthians 1:3-5, we read:

> He comes alongside us when we go through hard times, and before you know it, He brings us alongside someone else who is going through hard times so that we can be there for that person just as God was there for us.

Your Story
Some Positive Outcomes

If you've been following the writing exercises in previous chapters, you now have a good part of your story written: with setting, details, feelings, and perhaps connections to other stories in your life. It's time for some resolution. How did you get (or how are you getting) help for the difficult parts of your story?

First step

Answer some or all the following questions:

- What are some resources you used to find help? These can be books, websites, or organizations.
- Which people did you turn to for help?
- What role did God play in your story?

Example

Sharon might have answered the questions above like this:

- **What are some resources you used to find help? These can be books, websites, or organizations.** *I turned to the Bible, to mental health services, and to my church.*
- **Which people did you turn to for help?** *My husband, my family, counselors and therapists, my pastor.*
- **What role did God play in your story?** *He knew what I needed to heal: to return to the very thing I had run from, only in a helping capacity.*

You could go back to the chart you used in the last chapter to identify events. This time you can add resources, people, and God at strategic points.

Second step

Go back into your story and add content about the resources you used to get help, the people you turned to, and God's role in your story.

Example

For example, Sharon might have written:

When I was at my wit's end and just couldn't go back to my job for even one more day, I turned to my husband. I begged him to let me quit my job, but he said I had to stay. Finally, when I was worried that I might hurt myself or commit suicide, I turned to the mental health system and voluntarily entered a psychiatric ward. Ultimately, that caused even more hurt because no one thought I could be so upset about a commonly accepted practice. Finally, I turned to God. Or rather, God got hold of me and turned my life around.

Take a few minutes to write your version.

_____

_____

_____

_____

_____

_____

_____

_____

_____

_____

_____

_____

_____

_____

Looking for more resources and support?

Depending on what has stood out to you in this book—and where you are on the journey to "honestly assess the facts of our lives and begin to order truth" as Dan Allender put it—you might be tempted to skip over the questions and writing exercises. I completely understand.

Feel free to continue reading and come back to these exercises at the end of each chapter in a second reading.

And if you are interested in connecting with others on this journey, please go to my website, sydneysegen.com. There you'll find resources and personal access to my private Facebook group.

Section F
Where Is Jesus in PTSD?

"GOD, your God, is striding ahead of you. He's right there with
you.
He won't let you down; He won't leave you."
(Deuteronomy 31:6)

This is a very personal chapter for me. I'm the one who
experienced all three of the following stories, and I'd like you to
know the background.

When I was working my hardest to get a grip on PTSD, I
participated in two multi-week phone-in coaching groups that
were instrumental in my steps toward healing. The groups were
offered by the organization *Journey to Healing and Joy*[1], created by
author Marsha Means.

I must have been a terrible challenge for the coach who led
my groups! I just couldn't get over the hurt and injustice, and I
agonized on the phone every week. While the other participants
gave their progress reports, I was not making much progress at
all.

Actually, the concepts and teachings made sense to me
months *after* the groups ended and have figured tremendously in
my recovery to this point. So don't be too hard on yourself, or
compare your progress with others, if your path to healing seems
slow.

One of the questions my coach had for me when I described
a dream was, "Where was Jesus in that dream?" It was so
amazing to go back into a nightmare and see Jesus standing there,
bringing healing and peace to the entire situation.

In the following stories, I share three instances in which I've
applied this strategy. Visualization may be a completely foreign
concept to you, so if you don't fully understand the stories, that's

okay. Just take hold of what stands out for you. After all, we've tried to find healing by "understanding" and figuring things out. Let your heart grasp what it needs.

But if you do understand it, visualization can be a powerful healing tool; so I want to take some risk and share from my deepest experiences.

Perhaps you'll be able to see Jesus too.

Jesus in Repressed Memories
Sylvie, in her own words

"He kept His hand on me to protect me."
(Isaiah 49:2)

The baby girl lay stone still, wrapped in a filthy black shroud. She'd been left on the cold ground, all alone.

I knew her.

I had been trying to "save" this baby girl in recurring nightmares for more than 40 years. In the dreams, I would race through burning houses, rummage through cluttered cellars, chase after her through dense forests. Sometimes my sister would help me search; once, my sister saved the little girl. Through all those years, I never knew who the child was.

When I was 61 years old, the baby appeared to me in a dream. She came into a room that looked like a classroom, and started pointing to letters that ran in a border around the room. I understood that she was trying to spell out who she was. The baby was pointing at "R." She had been trying to communicate with me for a very long time, ever since "A."

I realized then that this little baby was the child from my dreams, and that somehow, she was "me." It slowly dawned on me that I had been searching for the real me for all those years, through all those recurring dreams. I spoke gently, and through tears, "You can stay with me. I will do my best to keep you safe."

She contemplated me for a minute, then went back out of the room.

After thinking about the dream, I realized I wasn't healthy enough to follow through on my promise, and the child seemed to know that. She stayed away for a few more years, until I resolved a sexual abuse situation I was working through at the time (see "An Unexpected Deliverance" in Section B).

As part of recovery from the abuse, I talked about this baby with my coach from *Journey to Healing and Joy*. She replied that, "When this baby wakes up, she will wake up in trauma. She's a part of you that split off at a very young age. The baby has been carrying the sexual trauma caused by your father for all these years."

Later, as I thought this over, I said to myself, "Well, at least this little one can wake up in a safe place." So I pictured a pink nursery with a white crib and soft carpet. I placed the tiny girl in the crib and peeled back the soiled, smelly shroud. I cleaned her with wet cloths. Hair, hands, tiny toes, all of her. Her skin took on a rosy glow, but her eyes were closed. I slipped her into a soft sleeper, swaddled her in a white blanket, and started rocking her. "I will hold you and love you back to life," I thought. Little did I know, that task was beyond my reach.

A week later, I described the nursery scene to my coach. She was silent for a bit, then quietly asked, "Where is Jesus in that nursery, Sylvie?"

I went back to the baby nursery in my mind. This time, Jesus was there, standing by the crib. I gave him the warm, limp baby. He cuddled her closely then took my place in the rocking chair.

"Jesus is healing you—both you and the little child that was hurt for so long," my coach explained. "Let Him do His healing work within you. It will take time."

Jesus is still healing me, and it's a long and painful process. He freed me from the worst of PTSD through prayers of deliverance. Yet remnants of PTSD still haunt me on many days and nights.

But God has the rest of my life in His hands. Together, we survive long days of flashbacks and tears. We laugh when I'm surprised by joy. We write about the pain. We listen to others' pain. I say, "Let's stick together through this."

We who have been shattered walk a treacherous journey to recovery. If we don't find peace on earth, we'll wrap ourselves with it in heaven.

Advice from Sylvie

If you are in a relationship with someone who has PTSD, please be patient. This person has no idea when a nightmare will strike or when some common sound, smell, or touch will trigger a terrifying flashback.

Generally, people don't get over PTSD; they learn how to handle it. These may be some of the hardest people in the world to love. But it's your love, support, and understanding that can return us to the healing path. Please be patient; PTSD is not done with us yet. What would we do if one day you decide you're done with us? When a PTSD episode hits, that's what we are so afraid of.

***

Insights from Sylvie's story
Helping traumatized people with or without PTSD

If you know people who have PTSD or have been through a trauma, you also know that they will have some difficult days. It's inevitable.

You can offer support to a person in distress in these (and other) ways:

- **Acknowledge** them. "Rough day? Want to talk?"
- **Listen**. "Would it help to tell me more about it?"
- **Follow up**. "How can we stay in touch?"
- **Refer** them to resources: counselors, support groups, and peer networks
- **Support** them within boundaries. "I'd love to chat until

two p.m., then ..." "Can you write me an email? I'm right in the middle of something, and I can't stop right now ..."

• **Ground them in reality.** "The past seems so real to you. But I'd like you to describe where you are right now."

If you find it difficult to hear what the person is sharing (trauma = atrocity), lovingly refer them to a pastor, counselor, or lay minister. Caring for people with PTSD isn't always easy. But then, God didn't call us to an easy life, did He?

Poetry as a Way of Healing

Some people find that reading or writing poetry can be healing. Have you ever tried to write a "Psalm of Lament" about your experiences? David wrote many of these, and you can find them in the book of Psalms in the Bible. The psalm below follows a very simple format. Read it, then see if writing a similar psalm might help you.

Address and introductory cry
1 Oh God, You are the all-knowing One who saw me as I was being formed in my mother's womb. You've known me all of my days, each one a gift from you. Today, I ask that You hear my prayer of hardship, healing, and hope.

Complaint or Lament
2 The evil that is in this world scorched me when I was still a babe, unable yet to speak or walk, and with no one to protect me. It singed me throughout my life, sometimes roaring up into infernos. It was insidious. I didn't know what it was or why the troubles kept coming.

Confession of Trust
3 But You saw me, You knew me, You were there for every shock, heartache, and trauma. Your steady love never wavered. You stood with me, You sheltered me, and sometimes You carried me so the flames could never burn me to ashes when I passed through the fire.

Prayer for Deliverance

4 Oh, please turn the flames around and send them away from me. Send Your Holy Fire to burn the evil out of my life once and for all. Obliterate the vile evil from my deep memories, from recent hurts. Set a wall of fire against any return of that old evil in any form.

5 You, the Creator of the world, can do this. You are doing it. I praise Your name for fighting fire with fire in my life. I rest now in the palm of your hand.

Amen

The divided self: dissociation

Sometimes a traumatic event splits the psyches of trauma victims. The trauma is so terrible that the victims can't—but must— endure it. What is a frail human to do? And how could a young child possibly endure?

During or after the trauma, to live any kind of life at all, the victims "forget" a period of time or bury a part of their personhood. This is what happened to Sylvie as a young child. She divided herself, or "dissociated" from the little child who was part of her—and who carried the pain of molestation to protect Sylvie.

Sylvie grew up to become a high-achieving educator, writer, and university department director. To attain these positions, she couldn't afford to consciously remember pain, blood, tears, and overstimulation from childhood molestation.

But Sylvie's body, intellect, and emotions remembered. They tried to make Sylvie aware of the missing parts of her personhood by providing "de ja vu" moments, making her suspicious or fearful in certain circumstances (for no reason she consciously knew), and through recurring nightmares of trying to save a little child.

Many people go through life never knowing the missing parts that would complete who they are. Some people who do discover these parts are often deeply shocked. This new knowing rocks their world. In fact, these parts, when discovered, often open up a whole new world of painful awareness. Sometimes, individuals are able to reintegrate their parts and become more whole.

Sometimes these people remain in pieces and do the best they can until they heal a little more and do a little better. The process can't be rushed, and "trying" to find missing parts is counterproductive. Just relax and keep focusing on healing. If this division of self is part of your story, God will reveal it to you one day. This is what happened to me.

No matter what, hold on to hope that life will improve, even if it feels like you're going backwards.

Jesus in Nightmares
Sylvie, in her own words

"My Presence will go with you, and I will give you rest."
Exodus 33:14 (Modern English Version)

"Where is Jesus in that nightmare, Sylvie?" my coach asked. I had just described in great detail a nightmare I'd had the week before in which I'd opened a door to a bedroom and saw my father molesting me as an infant. I woke up soaked in sweat and fear. I'd been sick to my stomach every day since the dream.

Dozens of flashbacks during that week played the nightmare movie over and over again in my head. Now my coach was asking me to voluntarily open the door to that terrifying room. She reminded me, "Jesus is always with us, so He was there."

In my mind, I cracked open the door—but it swung wide on its own. I took in the whole room at a glance. "It's the same room," I said, "But it's been completely cleaned."

In fact, the bed stood crisply made, the windows opened wide, and a clean sea breeze washed the air, riding in on rays of sunshine. The perpetrator was gone. I didn't see Jesus but I had no doubt He'd been there before me. "It's the same room, but totally different—because Jesus has been there. He cleaned up the mess," My heart pounded with awe and excitement! Jesus had cleaned up the room and replaced a night terror with a fresh-air memory I could see, feel, and touch.

Now, nearly a year later, I can remember I had the dream. But when I recall it, I don't see the old shadowy bedroom. I see the room that was renewed by Jesus. If I try, I can catch a glimpse of the original room, but I don't try. I don't want to see that. I want to see what Jesus did. I want to dwell on the clean, wholesome, miracle-memory of what Jesus did for me.

Advice from Sylvie

If—or when—you have terrifying dreams, you might feel like a victim all over again. But you don't have to feel that way. You can try inviting Jesus into your dream, then go back and look at it again. Maybe you'll see what Jesus has done, maybe not. Different strategies work for different people. But try something. You are worth it.

Look at the strategies below and choose what makes sense for you. Stand up to PTSD. Take away its control over you. Tell it who's boss (that's you).

***

Insights from "Jesus in Nightmares"
Ways to combat nightmares

- Tell your therapist or counselor about the nightmares and follow the advice.
- Ask about trying Imagery Rehearsal Therapy (IRT). Briefly, while you're awake, you change the ending to the nightmare so it is no longer upsetting. Then play the new dream over and over in your mind. According to research, this can reduce how often nightmares occur.
- Check with your medical doctor to make sure you don't have breathing problems at night that can instigate frightening dreams. (Trauma survivors as a group have a higher occurrence of sleep disorders related to breathing.)
- Ask your medical doctor or psychiatrist about medications that can reduce nightmares. Currently, a medication called "prazosin" has shown in some studies that it reduces or subdues nightmares and generally reduces PTSD symptoms. It has worked wonders for me, and now I get full nights of sleep.

• Develop a "containment plan," or list of things to do after a nightmare to feel safe again. For example, 1) Get out of bed and remind yourself you're in a safe place. 2) Read "comfort verses" in your Bible. 3) Pray for God to banish the nightmare from your mind and give you restful sleep the rest of the night. 4) Write down the nightmare, but with a positive ending.

Jesus in Flashbacks
Sylvie, in her own words

"Blessed are the eyes which see what you see."
(Luke 10:23, Modern English Version)

Nearly every day I have flashbacks of the moment I got PTSD. I saw my husband betray me right before my eyes. He either forgot I was there or didn't care. The flashbacks once ruined me for days, weeks, months. *Every time I relive the situation, I can't believe it is happening, even though it had happened in reality and in my mind a thousand times.* My heart pounds, I try and fail to hold back tears and sobs. I feel myself shatter, as I'm shattering now.

So the other day I decided to try the "Where's Jesus?" approach to these flashbacks, as I have successfully done with bad memories and nightmares.

I voluntarily went in my mind to the church sanctuary where the betrayal occurred, not to re-experience it, but to find out where Jesus was when the betrayal was going on. He is always with us, so I knew He'd be there. Whether I would see Him or not was another thing.

I took my seat in a pew near the front of the church and looked up at the worship band on the stage, where my husband was playing guitar. I watched my husband's eyes slide from me to a woman walking down the aisle next to me. I followed his line of vision. As I turned my head, she was passing right next to me. The scene might as well have been a wedding with my husband, the groom, beaming desire as he welcomed a bride who was both brazen and demur.

This time, though, as soon as the woman passed by me, I saw someone step into her place. Jesus suddenly stood where she had been a moment before. He held my gaze, as if to say, "Don't look; it's too painful for you to see. Keep your eyes on me." His white robes gleamed so bright I couldn't see anything else in the room.

While I still had a physical awareness of what was going on between my husband and his target of affection, I couldn't turn my head away from Jesus. While Jesus didn't prevent the betrayal, he steadily held my gaze with his own gentle eyes. He was there, turning my head and saying, "Don't look at the pain; look at me."

Now when the flashback invades my mind, I have a choice. I can leave my eyes on Jesus, or I can turn to see the betrayal. After practicing this for a couple of months, a sort of "shorthand solution" has emerged. It goes like this:

- I'm walking into the church.
- I see Jesus in his dazzling white robes.
- I focus on the Savior, and the room and pain disappear.

Advice from Sylvie

I am very visual, so the "where's Jesus?" technique works well for me. But it might not work so well for you. That's okay. We are all different, with different gifts. However, the outcome encourages me to say, "If you're suffering, and you think of a strategy that might work, and the strategy is biblical, of God, and reasonable— give it a try. Perhaps you'll experience God in a way that will comfort you and become a new strategy to handle flashbacks.

***

Insights from "Jesus in Flashbacks"
Why flashbacks are so upsetting

In a flashback, you literally reexperience the trauma. Your heart pounds, you become intensely fearful, and you "leave" the present as the past takes over once again. In addition, you have no control over flashbacks; you don't know when they will occur, and you can't force them to stop.

Sometimes a flashback plays over and over again in your head, making it extremely difficult to function at work, school, or home. Flashbacks take over your reality, your thinking, and your emotions, leaving you with no control at all.

Ways to combat flashbacks:

- Tell yourself that you are having a flashback, that what you're experiencing isn't really happening again. For example: "This is a flashback. This feels terrible and overwhelming. But this is not actually happening right now."
- Remind yourself that the worst is over. The event already happened and is in the past. "This happened in the past, not right now. The worst is truly over."
- Get grounded by touching something in the room, feeling the floor under your feet, become aware of sights, smells, and noises around you.
- Breathe deeply to get plenty of oxygen to your brain, which will help you reason better.
- Get support by calling a friend or asking someone nearby to sit and talk with you for a few minutes. "I'm having a really rough memory right now, could you talk with me for a moment?"
- Take the time to recover and regain your energy by taking a bath, resting, or doing something you enjoy.
- Play Christian or inspirational music.
- Eat mints or another tasty candy to help ground yourself.
- Crunch some ice chips; the cold and the crunchy sensation will help "wake you up."
- Be patient with yourself as you learn the best ways to cope with flashbacks. "I'm simply experiencing a

flashback. God, help me learn how to manage these memories and emotions."

How to help a friend or loved one who is having a flashback
If your friend "disappears," loses interest in what you both were doing, or seems agitated, they may be having a flashback. You can help most by staying calm. Say the person's name until they reconnect with you. Explain what happened, if you think that's what triggered the flashback, for example, "That young man looked a lot like John, didn't he?"

The person may respond by saying they had a flashback. Then you can just talk with them about the experience if that seems appropriate.

If the person has difficulty coming back to reality, these can be helpful steps to take:
- Ask if it's okay for you to hold their hand.
- Speak calmly and explain where you are.
- Offer the person something to eat or drink; swallowing and chewing can help ground the person.
- Ask the person if they are aware of the present surroundings. Don't ask about the event while they're in it. Distract and ground them. A therapist can deal with what's going on emotionally later. You want to simply help the person get back to a safe place.
- Encourage the person to walk with you or to put on a jacket or other piece of clothing, again to help ground themselves in reality.
- After the person seems to be fully aware, ask if they would like to talk about it. Ask who you could call for them.

Your Story
Where Is God in Your Story?

More than likely you've encountered God if you've been through trauma. He is always with us, and He was there with you when the shock and pain obliterated everything else that mattered. Some people call out to God for help at these times. Others become angry with God, that He would let such a thing happen. You may have some of both these feelings. But I'd like you to take a look back at your own story and think about places you did—or didn't—encounter God.

First step

Answer some or all the following questions. Sample answers are provided below.

- Does God enter into your thoughts, actions, feelings, or beliefs at various points of your trauma memory?
- Did you feel like communication with God was a two-way street? Did He communicate back to you in any way?
- Compare how you felt about God at the time of trauma and how you feel now.

Example

Sylvie might have answered the questions above like this:

- **Did God enter into your thoughts, actions, feelings, or beliefs at various points of your story?** *I cried out to God many times. I read the Bible for guidance, comfort, and direction. I knew that God knew what was happening to me and that He would take care of me.*
- **Did you feel like communication with God was a two-way street? Did He communicate back to you in any way?** *Sometimes God seemed to speak to me, especially*

once when He told me it was okay to leave my marriage. I believe God communicated with me through other people that He put in my path, and through my church, which embraced my messy pain with love and patience. God did show Himself to me, in the visualizations I described in this chapter.

- **Compare how you felt about God at the time of trauma and how you feel now.** *I couldn't understand why God could let this happen. I was so raw from the pain that I could only plead with God over and over to help my husband stop hurting me. Now, I know God was there, agonizing with me, waiting for me to build a new life with Him. I feel His comforting presence every time I go to sleep at night.*

Look back at the story you've been writing (if you have participated in the writing exercises) and perhaps just place checkmarks near incidents where you questioned God, or where you sensed His comforting presence.

Second step

Go back into your story and add facts and feelings about how God was there for you. If you didn't sense God's presence, don't worry. Trauma is trauma, and it can eclipse all that was good in our lives. But we journey through it, and I believe God shows Himself more and more as we heal. So keep an eye out.

Example

For example, Sylvie might have written:

I never thought of God being in the church when I saw my husband betray me. I never thought of inviting Him into my flashbacks. But I did! And the healing power I felt, and continue to feel, is nothing short of miraculous. The God of the Universe cared enough about every hurt to walk back through them again with me.

Take a few minutes to write your version of these answers.

As you do, make note of flashbacks and take opportunities to prayerfully try the visualization exercise yourself. In the process, and with God's loving help, you can discover your own "shorthand" tools to cope and grow.

_____

_____

_____

_____

_____

_____

_____

_____

_____

_____

_____

_____

_____

_____

_____

_____

_____

Section G
Summary of Symptoms and Strategies

Maxine was just drifting off to sleep when that old, frightening flashback popped into her head.

"I'm not going there," she said to herself.

Maxine focused her mind on the thought of Jesus in the room. His presence seemed so real that it crowded the flashback out of her mind. A sense of peace replaced the wave of anxiety. She pictured Jesus holding her warmly while she fell asleep. And she did.

Marcos was driving at top highway speed when suddenly a red sports car cut directly in front of him. He braked just in time. That's when the fear started.

The car accident that had killed his daughter claimed center stage in his mind. He started seeing the crash over and over again. "Get a grip," he told himself. "Literally." So Marcos focused his mind on the steering wheel he was holding so tightly. He felt the bench seat of the truck as it supported his legs and back. He made a mental check that he'd brought all the right things home from work. He surveyed the traffic around him.

As Marcos grounded himself, his heart slowly stopped racing. By the time he got home, he was self-composed but he still needed to tell someone about the flashback. So he did.

Sharon's neighbor was angry. He stood almost larger than life, too close to Sharon, and nearly yelled his words. Sharon started to disappear within herself, to dissociate as she had always done in the presence of anger. Then she thought, I can handle this.

Sharon quietly said, "I think we have to talk about this another time." The neighbor stopped yelling for a minute. Sharon said, "I'm going back into my house now, and I would like you to leave." She backed up a few steps, then turned to open her front door. The last she saw of her neighbor was his red face and clenched fists. By that time she was safely inside.

These three individuals have PTSD, but they've been working on strategies to contain it. In each case, they were able to stay in the present and take action against the power of the flashbacks. This had not always been so. It took years of hard work and practice.

Now these people are in control of PTSD; PTSD is no longer in control of them.

"Make sure I'm fit inside and out
So I never lose sight of your love,
But keep in step with you,
never missing a beat."
(Psalm 26: 2b-3)

Keeping in step with God is certainly the way to loosen the grip of PTSD. But keeping in step can be difficult. We must discern where He's leading, choose the way that puts us on His path, and navigate rough waters and barren terrain—just to stick with Him. Perhaps that's why the verse above is a prayer to God, not a statement.

This section concludes our journey through the traumas, struggles, and triumphs of several people who have PTSD or PTSD symptoms. These individuals have shared their stories because we all want you to know that, with God, anything is possible. We want you to be assured that many strategies are available (some in this book) to help loosen PTSD's grip on your life and to have hope again.

On the following pages, I've included strategies for helping you stay in step with God as you move toward healing and recovery.

• For individuals who have PTSD
• For people who have friends or family members with PTSD

I may not know you, but I wrote this book for you. My heart goes out to you. May God be with you in your continuing journey to finding hope after trauma and PTSD.

Sydney Segen, sydneysegen.com

PTSD is difficult to treat because it's stored throughout the brain.

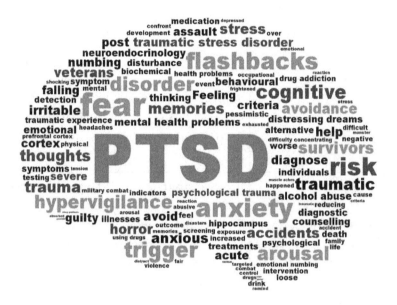

Try some of these strategies to combat PTSD symptoms:

Nightmares	Flashbacks	Withdrawing, isolating
Develop a containment plan to get back in control. For example: Turn on a light, pray out loud, remember that it was a dream, rewrite the nightmare so it becomes a dream with a happy ending.	Tapping: Use one hand to tap each shoulder, back and forth rhythmically as you describe the flashback out loud. Order the flashback to stop. Remind yourself that the event happened in the past and is over now.	Create a daily schedule and stick to it: 7 a.m. shower; 7:30 read devotion and have coffee; 8 a.m., take a walk. Meet a friend for coffee. Keep your doctor appointments. Join family or friends for meals, watching TV, etc.
Insomnia	Angry outbursts	Depression, poor self-image
Go to bed and get up at the same time every day. Don't drink caffeine after 10 a.m. Ask your doctor for medications. When you wake up, get up and do something until you're tired, then go back to bed.	Walk it off or work it off through exercise. Write down what makes you angry and why. See a therapist.	On bad days, try to get one or two things done. On good days, don't overdo it. Make lists of what you're good at, things you like to do, positive things others have said about you. Look in the mirror and tell yourself which physical characteristics are appealing.

Hypervigilance	Distorted feelings	Difficulty concentrating
When you see, hear, or smell something that reminds you of a past trauma, wait a beat before you react.	Reason with yourself: What else could I have done? I did everything possible to help.	Focus on a book, movie, or project as long as you can.
Notice how most other people are reacting and consider following their lead.	Check out your feelings with someone else to get the perspective of a person who is not so closely involved.	Try to increase your length of focus each time you come back to the activity.

This Is Your Loved One on PTSD

It's not always easy to be around people with PTSD, but your loyal love and friendship is what we need.

Use these strategies to help a friend who is having these symptoms:

Flashbacks	Sad, depressed, isolating	Needs someone who understands
Ask: Are you having a flashback? Want to talk about it? What do you think triggered it? Remind the person: That happened in the past, and now you're here, and you're safe with me.	Encourage the person to take up a hobby or take a class. Offer to meet with the person on a regular basis. Go fun places with your loved one. Explain that you're willing to just hang out and listen if that would be helpful.	Educate yourself on PTSD. Get to know what the person's body language indicates. Remember what the person has said in past conversations. Validate the person's feelings and actions.
Distrusting, afraid	**Despondent**	**Difficult to deal with**
Be someone the person with PTSD can count on. When you're on an outing, let the person choose where they want to sit. Avoid loud, possibly triggering outings. Do things that help the person feel safe.	Try to find out what has made the person feel so down. Listen and converse to see if this helps the person feel better. If the person mentions not wanting to live, or suicide, or ending it all, get professional help right away.	If you don't seem to be getting anywhere with someone who is upset, suggest you both take a break. Make sure that you're not burning yourself out trying to help the person with PTSD. Take time to do something fun or enriching for yourself and encourage the person to take "self-care" breaks, too.

- Remind your friend or relative that, with God's help plus time and treatment, they can get better.
- **Never ignore comments about death or wanting to die**. Contact the person's therapist or doctor for help or call the National Suicide Prevention Lifeline (1-800-273-8255) or 911 in an emergency.
- Encourage your loved one to talk about all treatment options with a mental health professional.

Your Story
Share It?

If you have followed along with the writing exercises, or if you are thinking about writing your story, the next step in healing is to share your story—when you're ready and where it's safe.

Telling your story can benefit you in a number of ways:

- Each time you tell it, it helps you process what happened.
- As you process your story, you'll begin to realize that the events happened in the past; they're no longer happening to you.
- As you start to grow through processing the events of the past, you will also gain courage, insight, and strength to change and move forward.
- If God is part of your story, you have opportunities to share with others what God has done in your life.

First step

Answer the questions below:

- Who is a "safe" person to tell your story to? This person should be someone who understands and supports you.
- Where are safe places to tell your story? In small groups? With others who may be suffering from events from the past?
- Would it hurt someone else if you told your story? You may need to change names and places to protect identities.
- If another person or other people were involved in your story, is it safe to share it with these individuals? I have, and the response was, "I had no idea you were going through all that."

Examples

- **Who is a "safe" person to tell your story to? This person should be someone who understands and supports you.** *At first I told my story only to trusted friends and a Stephen Minister (lay caregiver). Now I can tell it to anyone because I have processed it more fully, and it's not so upsetting to tell the story.*

- **Where are safe places to tell your story? In small groups? With others who may be suffering from events from the past?** *God will give you "divine appointments" with individuals or groups who will listen to your story and offer support. He may also prompt you to share with another person who is hurting. You can also offer this book as a way of supporting that person.*

- **Would it hurt someone else if you told your story?** You may need to change names and places to protect identities. *I went to great lengths in this book to change names, place names, and other details that might identify other people who were part of my story. The more public the place you tell it, the more careful you need to be.*

- **If another person or other people were involved in your story, is it safe to share it with these individuals?** *I have, and the responses were these: "I can see that you were in a terrible place. I'm sorry for my part ... By the way, some of the details were wrong." The last one made me laugh because it was my story and I had my details straight.*

Second step

Give it a try. Pray before you share your story. If you're going to read your story to someone, practice it so it comes out smoothly and understandably. If you're going to give it to someone to read, let them know that writing it was a very difficult process, and that reading it might be difficult too. No matter what the person's response, your story is your story; no one can convince you that you did not go through those terrible things.

Third step

Even if sharing your story was painful, give yourself a big hug. You've made a huge step in recovering from the effects of trauma and PTSD. Look ahead at the rest of your life because God has good things planned for you. You'll have another, happier story to tell one day.

I'd like to be the first to congratulate you! I'd love you to share your experience and your story on my website, sydneysegen.com, or confidentially on "Stories of Trauma, PTSD, and Hope," a Facebook page.

Thank you for taking this journey with me, and I pray for good things to come into your life so that your next story can be "Now I Have Hope Every Day."

Citations

Section A Introduction

[1]U.S. Department of Veterans' Affairs. *PTSD: National Center for PTSD* (https://www.ptsd.va.gov/public/PTSD-overview/basics/history-of-ptsd-vets.asp)

[2]Ibid. (https://medlineplus.gov/magazine/issues/winter09/articles/winter09pg10-14.html

Pornography: Deceiver, Destroyer—Dee-Dee

[1]Graham, Linda. *Bouncing Back.* (New World Library. 2013), 184, 186.

An Unexpected Deliverance—Sylvie

[1]Blazing Grace, "Porn, the Church, and What to Do About It." (http://www.blazinggrace.org/porn-the-church-and-what-to-do-about-it/)

Why Do Your Face Glow?—Maya

[1]Bessel A. van der Kolk, *The Body Keeps the Score: Brain, Mind, and Body in the Healing of Trauma.* (Penguin Books, 2014), 148.

[2]Langberg, Diane. *Suffering and the Heart of God: How Trauma Destroys and Christ Restores.* (New Growth Press, 2015), 267-268.

[3]Bessel A. van der Kolk, *The Body Keeps the Score: Brain, Mind, and Body in the Healing of Trauma.* (Penguin Books, 2014), 233.

[4]Schwartz, Arielle, Ph.D. The *Complex PTSD Workbook.* (Althea Press. 2016), 20.

Miraculous—Peg

[1]Turner, Kelly A., Ph.D. *Radical Remission.* (Harper One, 2014).

A Little Boy Burned—Maggie & Brian

[1]Allender, Dan B, Ph.D. *The Healing Path.* (WaterBrook Press, 1999), 194.

[2] Model Systems Knowledge Translation Center (www.msktcorg).

I Need You to See Me—Melanie

[1] American Society for the Positive Care of Children, (http://americanspcc.org/child-sexual-abuse/).

[2] Life Skills of [city unnamed to protect confidentiality], (please search "life skills" for more information).

[3] BrainyQuote.com. "Maya Angelou Quotes." (Xplore Inc, 2017). (https://www.brainyquote.com/quotes/quotes/m/mayaangelo1 33956.html).

All the Little Babies—Sharon

[1] Allender, Dan B. Ph.D. *The Healing Path*. (WaterBrook Press, 1999), 37.

[2] Langberg, Diane. *Suffering and the Heart of God: How Trauma Destroys and Christ Restores*. (New Growth Press, 2015), 76.

Section F

[1] *Journey to Healing and Joy* (https://journeytohealingandjoy.com/).

Resources

The information in *Hope after Trauma and PTSD: Making Sense of the Pain* comes from dozens of books, websites, articles, and course curricula. The sources listed here are especially helpful if you would like to learn more about a topic.

Allender, Dan B., Ph.D. *The Healing Path: How the Hurts in Your Past Can Lead You to a More Abundant Life.* (WaterBrook Press, 2015).

Allender, Dan B., Ph.D. *The Wounded Heart: Hope for Adult Victims of Childhood Sexual Abuse.* (NavPress, 2008 Edition).

Bruch, Debra. *Fractured Mind: The Healing of a Person with Dissociative Identity Disorder.* (Bruwicked Productions, 2016.

Carnes, Patrick J., Ph.D. *Out of the Shadows: Living with Sexual Addiction.* (Hazelden, Third Edition 2001).

CNN. "Roe v. Wade Fast Facts." 4/23/17 (http://www.cnn.com/2013/11/04/us/roe-v-wade-fast-facts).

Collins, R. Dandridge, Ph.D. *The Trauma Zone.* (Moody Publishers, 2007).

Covington, Ph.D. *A Woman's Way through The Twelve Steps.* (Hazeldon Publishing, 1994).

Gingrich, Heather Davediuk. *Restoring the Shattered Self: A Christian Counselor's Guide to Complex Trauma.* (InterVarsity Press, 2013).

Gonzales, Laurence. *Surviving Survival: The Art and Science of Resilience.* (W. W. Norton & Company, Inc., 2012).

Goodpastor, Kasey P.S. *History of PTSD: Every Man Has His Breaking Point.* (https://historyofptsd.wordpress.com/).

Graham, Linda M.F.T, *Bouncing Back: Rewiring Your Brain for Maximum Resilience and Well-being.* (New World Library, 2013).

Hall, Laurie *An Affair of the Mind,* "Post-traumatic Stress Disorder in Spouses of Sex Addicts," Part 1 of 3. (http://afteranaffairofthemind.com/ptsd/).

Hall, Laurie. *An Affair of the Mind.* (Focus on the Family, 1996.

Haugk, Kenneth C., Ph.D. *Christian Caregiving: a Way of Life.* (Stephen Ministries, 2012).

Haugk, Kenneth C., Ph.D. *Don't Sing Songs to a Heavy Heart: How to Relate to Those Who Are Suffering.* (Stephen Ministries, 2004).

International Society for the Study of Trauma and Dissociation, "Dissociation FAQ's," (http://www.isst-d.org/default.asp?contentID=76#dissam).

Koch, Ruth N, and Haugk, Kenneth C. *Speaking the Truth in Love: How to Be an Assertive Christian.* (Stephen Ministries, 1992).

Langberg, Diane. *Suffering and the Heart of God: How Trauma Destroys and Christ Restores.* (New Growth Press, 2015).

Levine, Peter A. with Frederick, Ann. *Waking the Tiger: Healing Trauma.* (North Atlantic Books, 1997).

Mastoff, Kelly. *Handling the Pornography Addiction: What's Wrong with a Few Dirty Movies Anyway?* (Kelly Mastoff, 2016).

Mcneill, Brian. *Medical Xpress.* "How pornography influences and harms sexual behavior," (https://medicalxpress.com/news/2015-01-pornography-sexual-behavior.html). January 27, 2015.

Means, Marsha. *Living with Your Husband's Secret Wars.* (Revell, 1999).

National Institute of Mental Health (https://www.nimh.nih.gov/health/topics/post-traumatic-stress-disorder-ptsd/index.shtml).

Morris, David J. *The Evil Hours: A Biography of Post-Traumatic Stress Disorder.* (First Mariner Books, 2015).

Scholten, Robert. *PTSD & Psalm Twenty-Three: Coming Up Out of PTSD's Trench.* (WestBow Press, 2016).

Shirer, Priscilla. *How to Recognize When God Speaks* (LifeWay Press, 2006).

Schwartz, Arielle, Ph.D. *The Complex PTSD Workook: A Mind-Body Approach to Regaining Emotional Control & Becoming Whole.* (Althea Press, 2016).

Struthers, William M. *Wired for Intimacy: How Pornography Hijacks the Male Brain.* (InterVarsity Press, 2009).

Thompson, Curt, M.D. *The Soul of Shame: Retelling the Stories We Believe About Ourselves.* (Intervarsity Press, 2015).

Tiede, Vicki. *When Your Husband Is Addicted to Pornography: Healing Your Wounded Heart.* (New Growth Press, 2012).

van der Kolk, Bessel A., M.D. *The Body Keeps the Score: Brain, Mind, and Body in the Healing of Trauma.* (Viking, Penguin Group, 2014).

Van Dijk, Sheri, M.S.W. *Calming the Emotional Storm: Using Dialectical Behavior Therapy Skills to Manage Your Emotions & Balance Your Life.* (New Harbinger Publications, 2012).

Viars, Stephen. *Putting Your Past in Its Place: Moving Forward in Freedom and Forgiveness.* (Harvest House Publishers, 2011).

Welton, Jonathan. *Eyes of Honor: Training for Purity and Righteousness.* (Jonathan Welton, 2012).

A portion of the proceeds from the sale of this book will be donated to the National Center for PTSD, an organization that provides information to the public and services to veterans.

About Sydney Segen

Easy, breezy, sparkly, fun. That's me—on good days.

But I've experienced trauma in my life and as a result have PTSD (Post-Traumatic Stress Disorder). So I also have other kinds of days.

On those days my veins feel filled with concrete; every move is an effort. My mind is dark, fighting off flashbacks. I lack confidence in myself and my future.

I want more of the good days. And I'm getting them.

Here's one of my strategies: I write.

This writing includes my story, others' stories, and some pretty rotten poetry. Then I think about how my story could help others get through their own difficult life stories.

Let's partner in writing our way through the hard times in life. I've listened to many people's stories, and I want to listen to yours. Tell it in bits and pieces or in a whole story start to finish—there's no right or wrong way.

What? You're not a writer?

That doesn't matter. We'll walk through the simple process together, step by step, and you'll have a true story when you're finished. In writing and sharing our stories, we can find healing.

www.sydneysegen.com

Would you like to join us?

I hope this book has been helpful to you, and helped you decide to pursue wholeness and growth.

One of the ways to continue your journey is to subscribe to my email newsletter and learn about our private Facebook group.

Continue your journey and join us by subscribing here: www.sydneysegen.com

CPSIA information can be obtained
at www.ICGtesting.com
Printed in the USA
BVHW041209141221
624028BV00012B/466